LEGAC

Wh

PRAY?

Lessons Learned in the School of Prayer

By B. J. Willhite

Hisway
Prayer Publications
P. O. Box 762
Jamul, CA 91935

WHY PRAY? *Lessons Learned in the School of Prayer Legacy Edition*

978-1-879545-18-2

Printed in the United States of America

Published by Hisway Prayer Publications

P. O. Box 762

Jamul, CA 91935

Publishers Note:

We all need heroes of the faith. We are very fortunate to have met Pastor Bob Willhite early in our ministry many years ago. Pastor Willhite became both our mentor in prayer and hero of faith. This great man's teachings on the subject of prayer radically impacted our lives and thousands of others throughout the U.S. and Internationally. Why Pray was written during a remarkable time in history when God was calling His people to prayer. (Ronald Reagan was President; the Berlin Wall was a focus point; and the Cold War was soon to end with the collapse of U.S.S.R.) National Call to Prayer began in Rockwall, Texas 30 + year and is still functioning to this day encouraging people to pray.

Our Reprinting this awesome book is to leave a Legacy of Prayer of this great man's teachings. You probably have never heard these principles of prayer anywhere else. They will encourage you, build your faith, and answer many of the questions you have had about prayer for a long time. You can listen to Pastor Bob's teaching at Hisway School of Prayer on most of the popular podcast platforms. Our prayer is that you will answer the call to prayer as we and thousands of others have.

One of the first principles that we learned from Pastor Bob was "If you have enough faith to pray...you have enough faith to move the hand of God".

God Bless You,
John & Kathy Casto
Hisway Prayer Publications

Dedication

To Velma, my wife and prayer partner
For over forty years

Contents

Foreword

From the moment I met B. J. Willhite, I sensed something different about him. At first, I couldn't quite put my finger on what that something was. Then it dawned on me: This slender, gray-haired gentleman with the deep, quiet spirit made me thirsty for God. And the more I learned about the man, the thirstier I got.

B. J. Willhite was born in northwest Arkansas in the days of the old tri-state Pentecostal camp meetings and grew up under the anointed preaching of men of God like Donald Gee and Raymond T. Richey. As a boy he saw platforms littered with crutches, braces and wheelchairs and heard joyful testimonies from the people who no longer needed them. Both of his parents were praying people. His mother literally died on her knees while in prayer, and his aunt died I the same manner.

At the age of nineteen, Bob Willhite fully committed his life to the Lord and to prayer. Hungry to know God he often prayed from the conclusion of the Sunday morning service until time for the evening service. Even military service did not weaken his habit of starting every day with prayer.

Bob married in 1947 and two years later he began preaching. Believing that preachers, of all people should pray, he committed himself to develop more discipline in prayer than ever before. Any pray he did, all through the twenty-eight years he pastored churches in Oklahoma, Missouri, Arkansas and Texas.

It was in 1978 during his pastorate at an Assemblies of God church in Kilgore, Texas, that I met B. J. Willhite. At that moment, neither of us realized that ours was a divine encounter. I was twenty-eight years old and, frankly, life wasn't making a whole lot of sense. I felt like a man without a country and I wasn't too sure that I even had a future. Most of my time was spend looking in my mind's rearview mirror, agonizing over what could have been.

You see, after Pastor Howard Conatser died in 1978, I was called to be the pastor of his three-thousand member church in Dallas, Texas. I had been serving as minister of youth and evangelism, and the people knew my heart. But right away, God let me know that I wasn't to accept the offer.

A man on the pulpit committee approached me with a proposition that went something like this: "Son, we're going to' triple your salary, put you on television, and make you rich and famous. You just preach sermons that bring people down the aisle and play your cards right, and we'll make you a success."

I could read between the lines, and I knew exactly what he meant. So I squared my shoulders, tried to swallow a baseball-sized lump in my throat and said, "Sir, I quit playing cards when I got saved." My forthright reply bought me a ticket back home to Kilgore, Texas.

Although I was graduating from seminary, and my wife and I had three small children by this time, I moved back into my parents' home. I sulked, moped and asked God a lot of questions – most of them beginning with how, when, or why.

But in the middle of my depression and confusion, I met Bob Willhite, who invited me to conduct a revival in his church. Soon afterward, as I was shaving one morning, the Lord spoke these words in my spirit: "B. J. Willhite is to be your pastor." Ever since that time, Bob Willhite has remained my pastor; not to give me orders or pressure me, but to be my friend, counselor and advisor.

The revival I conducted for Pastor Willhite and his praying people lasted seven weeks, and we saw five hundred teenagers saved – including the entire senior class of one of the local high schools. But the greatest conversion that happened during that revival was my personal conversion to become a man who was more interested in prayer than anything else in life. It came about like this.

One evening I remarked, "Pastor Willhite, I understand you are a man of prayer."

"That's right," he said, "I Pray. For over thirty years I've been rising early in the morning to pray."

Masking my excitement I asked, "While the revival is going on, would you let me come pray with you in the mornings?"

"Why, yes," Bob agreed, "I'll pick you up in the morning at 5:00."

I have to confess that when 4:15 rolled around the next morning and my screeching alarm clock went off, I didn't feel one ounce of anointing to pray. Actually, if I hadn't promised Pastor Willhite that I'd be ready at 5:00, I probably would have gone right back to sleep. Somehow I managed to shower, shave, get dressed and remain standing upright until Bob's Oldsmobile Cutlass pulled into the driveway.

As we rode to the church that morning before dawn, I didn't have any idea what God was going to do in my life, but a sense of fulfillment and excitement in my spirit told me that I was answering the most vital call of my ministry – the call to pray.

In January 1979, Pastor Willhite shared a vision with me. He had just arisen from his knees and sat down at his desk when he heard the beginning of a radio broadcast – without the aid of a radio! He listened in amazement as a booming bass voice sang the theme song 'God of Our Fathers." Next, the opening announcements were made and the program began. At that moment, the concept of a 300,000 member prayer army crystallized in his mind: an army that would be enlisted instructed and inspired to pray through a national call to prayer.

Soon after this, I began traveling as an evangelist. One morning while I was in prayer, the Holy Spirit revealed truths about the Lord's prayer that were to revolutionize my prayer life and ministry. Months later while I was in Canada conducting a youth revival, the Lord spoke in my spirit and said, "Go to Rockwall and establish My people there."

Rockwall, Texas, a town with a population somewhere around eleven thousand people, is perched on a ridge overlooking Lake Ray Hubbard, some twenty-five miles east of Dallas. It is a small town in the smallest county in Texas. If God had commanded, "Fall off the face of the earth, "I don't think I could have been more astonished. Actually, at the time, the two orders would have appeared to be somewhat synonymous.

I moved my family to Rockwall and started applying the principles God had taught me about growing a church. We began Church on the Rock (COTR) in 1980 with thirteen people, not knowing that within a few years we would have well over five thousand active members, several dozen staff members and almost four hundred home cell groups.

But what about my friend, B. J. Willhite, the man God had said would be my pastor? What was happening in his life? I discovered that Bob, consumed by the mandate God had given him, had resigned his church. He was traveling, teaching on prayer, airing programs on twenty-six radio stations and working fervently to raise up the prayer army. I contacted him and in 1983 Bob moved to Rockwall to become COTR's minister of prayer. The vision burning in his heart of a 300,000 member prayer army soon ignited in my heart as well.

We knew in our spirits that God wanted to use COTR as His launching pad for National Call to Prayer. Together we labored to raise up and train faithful intercessors. I put in writing the revelation on prayer God had given me and started conducting prayer clinics in major U.S. cities. But how could two relatively unknown men raise up a prayer army of 300,000 intercessors? How could we help launch the prayer assault that would storm the gates of hell?

Over and over, God has confirmed to B. J. Willhite and me His promise that "promotion cometh neither from the east, nor from the west, nor from the south" (Ps. 75:6, KJV). Promotion comes from God. Within four years, we have seen the prayer message taking root and bearing fruit in hungry hearts and obedient congregations all over the country. Opportunities have come to teach the prayer message on nationwide television networks; my book on prayer, *Could You Not Tarry One Hour?*, published by Creation House in 1987, is a best-seller. Over 150,000 intercessors are enrolled in the prayer army, which is growing at the rate of ten thousand per month.

Now God has moved another giant step closer to His goal of calling our nation and our world to prayer and repentance. In September 1988, B. J. Willhite established the National Prayer Embassy in Washington, D.C. The center is the first link of a giant, globe-spanning prayer chain. I have pledged Bob my full support along with the leaders of virtually every major prayer ministry, including Gary Bergel, Vonette Bright, David Bryant, Dick Eastman, Corinthian Boone and Glen Sheppard – intercessors who have for years recruited Christians to pray.

Because the National Prayer Embassy serves as the nerve center for the nation's prayer, intercessors will now be able to pray as a united body in a more intelligent, efficient manner. Bob believes that by the end of 1989, the embassy will be in daily contact with hundreds of thousands of intercessors all over the world. Exciting? Of course! Humanly possible? No way. This miraculous chain of events has been inspired by the Lord and is empowered by prayer.

Bob Willhite's example helped move my prayer life from desire to discipline to delight. Take this godly man's teaching and devour it. The truths he shares in this book will inspire you to pray as never before!

Larry Lea, Senior Pastor
Church on the Rock
Rockwall, Texas

Introduction

Why Don't Christian Pray?

Never before in this age has there been a greater interest in prayer. The "you are there" news media has brought into our homes all the religious cultures of the world. What is their common goal? The search for God. And the single most consistent act in this search is *prayer.* From the privacy of our living rooms we can see and hear the Buddhist, the Hare Krishna, the Hindu, the Muslim, even the pope himself and some two dozen Christian television evangelists pray. (Certainly I don't mean to equate prayer offered to graven images with that made to the God of Abraham, Isaac and Israel – the God and Father of our Lord and Savior, Jesus Christ.)

What does this universal search for God reveal? It's the result of what Saint Augustine called the "God-shaped vacuum in man"; the human heart cries out in anguish until it is filled with God. Our souls innately yearn for fulfillment through communion with God. If the soul's longing is not satisfied by communion with the heavenly Father, it will feast on a compelling counterfeit – whether it be a graven image or the most ruthless and unforgiving of idols: one's self.

Most professing Christians know they ought to pray but, for whatever reason, they do not. When they do pray, they don't really understand what they're doing or how it works.

Recently at a pastors' conference in Dallas, Texas, a group of approximately two thousand pastors was asked some pointed questions about their prayer life. Ninety-five percent said they prayed five minutes or less per day. When I heard this, I asked the obvious question: Why did such a high percentage of these fundamentalist pastors pray so little? Surely these pastors have read the Scriptures, yet their practice is so telling. Having been a pastor for thirty-four of my thirty-nine years in the ministry, I know you cannot lead people to a place where you are not prepared to go. If pastors are not praying, neither are the people.

I have the kind of mind that cannot rest until I find satisfactory answers to my questions. So I began to pray and search for answers. As I did, I reached some rather startling conclusions – which ultimately moved me to write this book.

I've seen that many of God's children do not pray, except in emergency situations or when they are asked to do so, because they are not sure their prayers make any real difference. Think about it. Are you sure your prayers affect the outcome of things? If you answer as most Christians do, you will say: "I'm not sure. At times I think they do; at other times I think they don't."

Most Christians I talk to believe that prayer makes a difference. They will affirm their faith in the fact that "prayer changes things" but they're not so sure that their own prayers do. This feeling seems to be born of inferiority rather than humility. Unless one can believe that his or her prayers really make a difference that person will not pray consistently. He or she will leave the praying to others who seem to pray effectually.

As a result of years of dealing with people on a one-to-one basis, I'm convinced that m any Christians are fatalistic in their view of the future. They believe that what is to be, will be – everything that happens is the will of God. It is easy to see why anyone having such a philosophy would not pray consistently: prayer would be a total waste of time for them.

Now many deny believing such a thing, but actions speak louder than words. If we say we believe prayer changes things and do not pray, we sin: "To him who knows to do good and does not do it, to him it is sin." (James 4:17). On the other hand, the person who o feels that prayer doesn't make any real difference in the outcome yet prays anyway is acting hypocritically.

Why such confusion? Because these believers have incomplete information that doesn't jibe with personal experience. Some respected person has told them, "God answers prayer." Thought this is a true word, He does not answer every prayer. A preacher has said, "God still heals – all you have to do is pray and believe." Yes, God does heal at times but not every time we pray. A person believed to be a man of God has told them, "If you need a miracle, pray and you will see a miracle." Yes, God may send a miracle in response to some prayers, but He may not.

If someone has prayed and been disappointed in prayer ("I prayed and nothing happened"), that person may begin to question God's love and quit praying consistently.

Then, ultimately, some people don't pray because they are dominated by doubt. The problem is often more self-doubt (I can't pray effectually) than doubt that God exists or that He can do anything He has committed Himself to do.

But we Christians are called to pray. When Jesus went into the temple in Jerusalem and cast out those who were making the temple a house of merchandise, He said, "My house shall be called a house of prayer..." (Matthew 21:13). I know Jesus would not want His house called a house of prayer unless that is what it is. We are not in the dark about His will concerning His house. He wants prayer to be the primary characteristic; He wants His house to be known as a place of prayer.

Today the temple of God is not a building. The church meets in a building, but we believers are the temple of the Holy Ghost both corporately and individually (see I Corinthians 3:16; 6:19). Paul said that we are a "habitation of God in the Spirit" (Ephesians 2:22). Knowing that your heart is the dwelling place of the Holy Spirit, consider what Jesus said, "My house (dwelling place) shall be a called a house of (characterized by) prayer."

Now notice the next phrase of Jesus: "...but you have made it..." You have made it something other than what AI intended it to be. Even the casual observer can see that in many churches more time is devoted to music, preaching and announcements than to prayer. If we have made His dwelling place something other than He intended, then we can make it what HE wants it to be. How? Before I answer let me say that it will not become a house of prayer until you make some decisions about the matter. Those decisions must be based on an understanding of what the Lord really wants. Once you set yourself in agreement with heaven on the matter, you can do two things: First, repent for having made His house something other than what He wants. Second, ask Him to help you become what HE desires.

My parents and the preachers that peppered my childhood set me on a path that I call the school of prayer. Though older and/or wiser pray-ers have taught me many of the lessons I've learned, the Holy Spirit has been my major professor.

Throughout my sixty years on earth, I've taken many questions to Him: Why did I sometimes pray with what seemed to be much faith – and yet I saw no answer? Why, at other times, did I pray with what seemed little faith – and I received an immediate answer? Why did God want me to pray? Did He not have all power in heaven and in earth? Did He not have a will about everything that made a real difference? If He had a will and all power, why didn't He just do what He willed and had the power to do?

Knowing that God's Word says, "Seek Me and you shall find Me," I began to seek Him wholeheartedly. As I did, He revealed certain truths to me that satisfied my desire to understand.

Some of the lessons God has given me concerning prayer are in the pages of this book. As I write, I pray that these truths will help the reader as much as they have helped the writer.

Chapter One

Lord, Hear My Prayer

I grew up in a little box house on the bank of Leatherwood Creek in northwest Arkansas. Just five small rooms and a path. No electricity. No running water- except the creek. We were poor, even by the standards of those days, yet we were rich in the things that really matter. My parents knew how to pray and they prayed. Every time we sat down at the table to eat, though the fare may have been meager, Dad always gave thanks to God and prayed for His guidance. We worshiped in a church supplied by lay preachers from Eureka Springs. About once a year, a real preacher would come and hold a revival meeting. At one of those revival meetings, I was saved. Feeling the conviction of sin and knowing I was lost and needed Jesus. I walked down the aisle, weeping and asking God to forgive me and come into my heart. Before the week was over, Hugh Weston (known as the worst sinner in the community) was born again, as was nearly every kid in our one-room school.

I preached my first sermon during those meetings—on my way home from school. My school mates were my audience; an oak stump was my pulpit; a log was the altar. When I gave an invitation to "get saved," the children came forward to the log altar. Even the school teacher, Mr. Fagin, got "on fire" for Jesus, making the school day seem like a continuation of church. Those were glorious days, and God chose that time to give me my first personal answer to prayer.

Lord, Hear My Prayer

It had been raining that warm, early spring day and I could hardly wait for school to be dismissed. I knew the bullhead catfish would be biting in Leatherwood Creek. It was a mile from the school to our house and I think I ran all the way home. I opened the door and rushed in. "Mom, where are the fishhooks?" I yelled. But nobody answered. I'm not sure, but she was probably visiting Mrs. Hilton, our nearest neighbor. I looked everywhere for those hooks. I had to find them, but I couldn't. They weren't to be found anywhere. Finally, I stopped right in the doorway between the kitchen and the living room, looked up toward heaven and called out loudly, "Lord, help me find the fishhooks!"

Now before the echo of that prayer had left the room, I knew where the hooks were—on top of the safe. (For my younger readers, that is not where we kept our money, but where Mom kept the dishes and the non-perishable food.) There they were, where I could hardly see them, in a little paper bag. folded down.

"Baby Faith"

I cannot remember anything about fishing that afternoon. I'm not even sure I went, but I've never forgotten that God heard my prayer. When I look back, the fishhooks don't seem to be a very important issue or need. But my Father used them to teach me an important lesson in prayer: God takes us where we are and patiently teaches us that He loves us and will respond to our prayers—even I f they don't seem very important.

Have you ever noticed how new Christians seem to receive an answer to every prayer? They pray, "Lord, let that light turn green; I'm running behind schedule." Like a miracle, it turns green. Then they pray, "Lord, I need a parking place near the covered walk' it's raining." And, sure enough, there it is. God gives them a parking place not ten feet from the canopy.

I used to wonder about this. Was it because they had such great faith? Or was it because they had such little faith? I believe the latter is the case. Our Father takes us right where we are. He knows our faith is little and that it rests more in what He does than in who He is.

Think of this in terms of a baby. Babies are selfish and self-centered. We expect them to be. Our heavenly Father expects us to be normal., and it normal for a baby to be a baby. But babies are expected to grow up at some point in time. It has been my experience that, painful though it is, God will see to it that we grow. There will come a time when we will pray about some little matter and nothing will happen. There will be no answer—not because we have no faith or have failed God in some way—but because our Father wants us to see beyond ourselves.

Growing Faith

My dad, who died at age ninety-two while I was writing this book, was a faithful Christian all of my life. When I was young, the church service usually included testimonies during which I would often hear Day say, "I never got serious with God about anything for which I did not get an answer. "But there came a day in Dad's life when he got serious and nothing happened. He prayed very earnestly and there was no answer, at least not the answer he expected/

I had just gotten home from the Sunday evening service at my church in south Arkansas when the telephone rang. My brother Laverne was on the phone. He said: "Bob, Mom has had a stroke or something. She is in the hospital. You had better come."

I got my family in the car as soon as I could and drove as fast as the roads would allow to get to Mom's side. When I arrived a few hours later, she was still breathing but unconscious. They told me that she had been praying at the church altar when it happened. A blood vessel had burst in her head. A little while later she went to be with her Lord.

Dad was grieved because of Mom's death, but there was another matter that troubled him. He had prayed and God had not responded. Some time later he said to me, "Son, I don't know whether I have enough faith to be saved."

I hope you can understand what I am trying to say. Faith must have a transition at some point in life. I must rest in who God is, not in what He does. He is God—even when He does not respond to our prayer. He does not answer every prayer we pray: not because He does not have the power, but because it would not be the best to do so.

It was Abraham we said, "Shall not the Judge of all the earth do right?" (Gen. 18:25). The question was meant to be rhetorical. Of course, God will always do the right thing. How thankful I am that He has not answered all of my prayers. The world would be in quite a mess if He granted every request. We are just not smart enough to tell God what to do. Of course we want our way, but if we are wise we will say with Jesus, "Nevertheless not My will, but Yours, be done." (Luke 22:42)

Chapter Two

With All My Heart

Did you notice that I cried out to the Lord for the fishhooks loudly? When I was very young I learned that God isn't nervous or easily startled.

Though our house could hardly hold our family—Mon, Dad, and five boys—the visiting preachers often stayed with us. One of those men really impressed me with the intensity of his prayers. Fred McConnell would go down into the little valley north of our house and pray, usually in the late afternoon before the service. Well, Brother Fred prayed so loud that you could hear him a mile away. Was he ever sincere!

Do you know that a lot of people believe that the only way to pray is quietly or silently? The possibility of silent prayer never entered my mind as a child. Everyone prayed out loud, and often with tears.

I'm not saying that we must pray aloud to be heard; we must pray with emotions to be heard.

I did not know then that this was, in fact, the way Jesus prayed—aloud and with emotions. Hebrews 5:7 says of Jesus: "Who, in the days of His flesh....offered up prayers and supplications, with vehement cries and tears to Him who was able to save Him from death, was heard..." The Word of God assures us that our high priest can be "touched with the feeling of our weaknesses" (Heb. 4:15,KJV). Feelings—emotions—do touch our Lord.

An Old Testament story illustrates this fact very well (2 Kings 20:1-6). King Hezekiah was sick unto death. In fact, God sent Isaiah to tell Hezekiah, "Set your house in order, for you shall die." Notice Hezekiah's response to this prophetic utterance: He turned his face to the wall and prayed—and wept bitterly. Verse 4 says that before Isaiah had gone out of the middle court, God spoke to him again and said, "Return and tell Hezekiah....: "I have heard your prayer, I have seen your tears; surely I will heal you...and I will add to your days fifteen years." Our Father was moved by Hezekiah's tears, touched by his emotions.

David knew the importance of tears. Psalm 56:8 says, "Put my tears into Your bottle." It may be that the golden vials John saw in heaven contain the tears of the saints offered up with their prayer. (see Rev. 5:8)k

Emotions are a vital part of prayer. No one told me that when I was a boy, but it was frequently demonstrated by those close to me who prayed. Their needs were great; they felt them deeply and prayed about them fervently. As James 5:16 says, "The effectual fervent prayer of a person in right standing with God releases tremendous power" (author's paraphrase). Effectual prayer is fervent. The greater the need, the more intensely we feel it.

To me, it would not be emotionally or psychologically honest to come before God with a religious prayer. (O Thou most high God, Creator of heaven and earth, hear the plea of this Thy humble servant as I calmly communicate with Thee about this emergency.) To be honest, we should lift up our voices with strong crying and tears.

It may have been my mother who demonstrated this most clearly to me. I never heard her speak the name of Jesus with her voice breaking and her eyes filling with tears. She was so precious. In fact, she prayed me into the ministry.

The Call

When I was five years old one of the lay preachers at church, Uncle Bill Terril, asked me, "What are you going to be when you grow up?" I still remember my response: "I'm going to be a 'holy-roller' preacher." I'm not sure I knew the meaning of the term, but that's what they called Uncle Bill, and I wanted to be whatever he was.

The real call to the ministry came years later, when God spoke to me out of the wind.

By December 1941 electricity had come to Eureka Springs. We had a refrigerator, a washing machine, an electric pump in our well—and a radio. I remember hearing President Roosevelt on the radio that Sunday afternoon when he detailed the Japanese attack of Pearl Harbor.

I was thirteen. My oldest brother, Bill, was twenty-three and newly married with one child. Laverne was seventeen, Ronnie was nine and Bud, the 'baby', was five. Of course, Bill was called right away to report for induction into the armed forces. We never knew why he didn't pass his physical. He had never been seriously ill in his life. Mom always believed God had answered her prayer—she wanted her grandchild to have a father at home.

In November 1942 Laverne went into the Air Force and we did not see him again until December 1945, when he returned home safe and sound. Mom was also sure that God had spared his life, and the rest of us agreed.

During the war, my parents moved to eastern Oklahoma. After the war, in June 1946, Velma, my girlfriend at the time, my brother Bill and his wife, Veda, and several other young people from the church rented a small outboard motorboat for a Sunday afternoon outing. We crossed to the south side of Spavinaw Lake where we enjoyed a picnic. When it looked like rain, we set out for our cars on the north shore. There must have been seven or eight of us—far too many for that small boat, especially in the rough weather we faced before we could get across the lake. Only three of us could swim, and there were no life jackets in the boat. When I realized the grave danger we were in, I cried out to the Lord for help.

Suddenly, out of the storm, I hear a clear voice. I knew it was God as He simply said, "Will you preach My Word?" I realized the question was addressed to me. I'd long since ignored that childhood intention to be a preacher. As a teenager I acquired other ambitions—but in that moment all other aspirations vanished. I will never forget my response to that whirlwind voice. Thinking this was the condition under which God would spare us, I responded with a loud voice, "Yes, Lord, I will." My mother's prayers had been answered. I'd been called to preach, though it was still some months before I wholeheartedly accepted the call.

One month later, July 14, 1946, I turned eighteen and immediately joined the Army. Three months later, after basic training, I was stationed at Letterman General Hospital in San Francisco. Before long, I had just about forgotten my commitment to preach God's Word. Army life and the bright lights of San Francisco had me under their spell. God—or the church—was not a part of my life. But—Mom was praying.

Knowing I was not where I needed to be with God, Mom had a real heaviness for me. At the beginning of a church service later that year Mom got the attention of her pastor, L. R. Bell. She was weeping and between sobs she told him, "I have such a burden for Bob."

Everyone in that little country church prayed. At the moment they started to pray, I suddenly felt an urge to go to church—to get my life back in tune with God.

I had received a letter from Pastor Bell telling me about a church in the Fillmore district of San Francisco. That being the only church I had heard about, I made my way there. I go on the streetcar and rode to Geary Avenue, two blocks from the church. Walking those two blocks, I was stopped twice by prostitutes. But my conviction to get right with God was so strong that they were no temptation.

I cannot tell you what message the pastor, Leland Keyes, preached that night. I just wanted him to get through the sermon and give me the opportunity to come back to God. Finally he did—and I did. At that altar my life totally changed. Suddenly, I wanted to do nothing more than serve the Lord and do His will. My mother's fervent prayer had been answered again.

CHAPTER THREE

Father Knows Best

As a young man, I learned several truths that laid the groundwork for later insights God gave me into prayer. Remember, He takes us where we are and increases out knowledge of Him as we grow in Him.

When that trip to the altar changed my life, prayer became very important to me. I started to pray about everything. I often stayed in the prayer room at Glad Tidings Tabernacle all day on Sunday—from the end of the morning service until the beginning of the evening service. Over the next four months, I noticed that every time I went into that prayer room a woman was there—crying out to God as if her heart would break. Sometimes I would overhear her prayer. Over and over she would say, "Lord, save India. Lord, save India." Hour after hour this was her prayer.

Until that time, I had never heard anyone pray for a nation to be saved. But as I studied the Word, I noticed that in Psalm 2:8 the Father, speaking to His Son, says, "Ask of Me, and I will give you the nations for Your inheritance, and the ends of the earth for Your possession." This prophetic psalm reveals the Father's will concerning the world and its nationalities. To the Son He said, "I will give them to You."

I realized that if the Son was instructed to pray in this manner, we should pray this way too. Second Peter 3:9 says that God is "not willing that any should perish but that all should come to repentance." And in his great revelation, John say a time when the kingdoms of this world would become the kingdoms of our Lord and of His Christ (Rev. 11:15). It is the will of God that all ethnic groups be saved; the blood of Jesus fully paid the price for the redemption of all.

There is but on thing left to be done. We, the church, must rise up and possess everything the Lord Jesus purchased. We must pray—with the commitment that we will be the instrument through which His will is done—and we must obey. Someone has said, "We must pray as if everything depends on God and work as if everything depends on us." If we are not willing to be used by God to answer our prayers, we may be praying in vain.

One Friday morning in 1979, I was praying with the men of my church and suddenly I was overwhelmed with a burden for China. My heart broke as I thought of that land's spiritual darkness and oppressive government. As I prayed, the tears flowed down my face; I was sure that I had entered into the heart of God about China , feeling in a small measure as He did. At some point, I prayed in language which sounded oriental to me. It was like being a Chinese Christian crying to God for deliverance from oppression.

I've learned that when one feels such a burden, one can be sure that others who are in tune with God are feeling the same load. Knowing this can keep one encouraged—and humble.

I discovered later that a group called Operation Sunrise had been praying for China for twenty-five years. I entered the picture late, but the time for change had come. Extraordinary prayer was offered up that Friday, and within a matter of days relations between the United States and China improved. Doors were opened to travelers from the West. Trade was reestablished. The government of China soon offered to restore to mission boards property that had been confiscated by the communists when they had taken over the government twenty-five years earlier. Bibles, its not legally permitted, were once again tolerated.

Now, some years later, Bibles are being printed in China. What a fantastic answer to the prayers of God's people.

My commitment to pray for the nations was established because of the lesson I learned in the prayer room of Glad Tidings Tabernacle in San Francisco. For the first time I realized that prayer could reach beyond our own personal needs.

Putting Jesus First

Earlier, I mentioned Velma, the girlfriend who was with me in the boat when I received my call to preach. Velma was no casual friend. We had dated through high school and were unofficially committed to each other when I went into the Army. When I made my new commitment to the Lord, I wrote to tell her what had happened. In that letter, among other things, I said some strong words: "You no longer have first place in my life. Jesus is first and you will be second."

Not many days later, I received her response: "Dear Bob, I have been dating another guy. Let's you and me just be friends..."

Words to that effect would have normally hurt me terribly, but to my surprise, I was not hurt, angry or disappointed. I knew Jesus was first in my life and that, if this was the girl for me, He would work things out. I would only keep writing her, telling her about my walk with Jesus and how good He was to me.

On December 31, 1947, I was discharged from the Army, having fulfilled my commitment to the government. When I returned home, I did not run to see Velma. I truly felt the matter was in God's hands. If anything was to come of this relationship, He would have to move on her heart.

Our little church was having a revival meeting at that time—with an old-time Pentecostal preacher whom everyone called Hallelujah Hopkins. Brother Hopkins was not such a good preacher. In fact, he could hardly read, but he and his wife knew how to pray, and the Holy Spirit was moving. Many nights, after the church service was over and they had retired to their little homemade trailer, they could be heard praying into the wee hours of the morning. Just about every reprobate in the community was saved—not because of Brother Hopkins' preaching, I'm convinced, but because of his and others' prayers.

Wednesday afternoon of the week of my return from the Army, Velma called and asked if I would see her before the evening service. As we sat in my car, she spoke "I have decided to commit my heart to Jesus tonight. I'm going to college this spring semester. Will you marry me when I finish college?"

Wow! Was I surprised! But I had a quick answer for her. "No, I won't." I paused for a little effect. "But I will marry you just as soon as we can arrange it."

I knew God had worked His will. Ten days later we were united in holy matrimony. That was over fifty years ago, and we have never had a serious quarrel.

I had learned a very important lesson. If you put God first in your life, everything will fall into its proper place. I was not aware at that time that Jesus had taught this principle to His disciples. In Matthew 6:33 He said, "But seek first the kingdom of God and His righteousness, and all these things shall be added to you."

Twice in this sixth chapter of Matthew Jesus said that your heavenly Father knows what you need (vv.8, 32). And in saying this He implied that it was not necessary for us to keep asking Him to meet our needs. Later I will deal in detail with this principle, having learned more about prayer and how it works as I grew older.

God is Good

I preached my first sermon on my twenty-first birthday, July 14, 1949. After a year of preaching at the Piney School, near Jay, Oklahoma, I decided to go to Bible school. But the coming of the Lord seemed so near that I quit after one year. I then became pastor of a small church in southern

Missouri. I will never know why those people called me—I was so young and inexperienced. I stayed there thirty months before moving on to another church in Monett, Missouri. There I learned one of my most valuable lessons in the school of prayer. One Sunday afternoon I was praying at the church, just waiting on the Lord, drawing near to Him. I had just said to Him, "Lord, I want to ask You to do this thing for me, but I don' t feel worthy..."

Suddenly, He was there, standing on my right. My head was down and my eyes were closed, but I knew He was there. I was afraid to open my eyes, knowing that if I saw Him, I would die.

Then He spoke, kindly but firmly, "Son, whatever gave you the idea that I bless you because you are good, I bless you because I am good."

Along my journey I had correctly understood that sinners were saved by grace only. But then I'd picked up the erroneous idea that after one was saved, God's blessings were conditional. That is, I thought that we had to merit any further manifestations of His goodness toward us. I was always trying to make myself worthy of His blessings, and I was always falling short. My Lord's statement that day about His goodness changed my whole life and ministry.

His statement to me may not seem very important to one who was raised in a "grace" church, but this was not a doctrine of my church. This little Pentecostal fellow was hearing this word for the first time—and it was coming directly from God. It was a revelation from God and it was real. I had experienced His grace, but I had not understood its limitlessness. Now I did.

After I'd heard His message, I began to see this truth everywhere in the Word. I could come before Him with confidence in His goodness and pray boldly at "the throne of grace" (Heb. 4:16)—not a throne of judgment at which all comers are scrutinized by the all-seeing eyes of the judge of the universe. His throne is a throne of giving. Only one thing is required: an attitude of faith that believes that God is and that He can and that He loves us enough that, according to His will, He will do it.

We come before Him, not with a righteousness that we have sewn together with fragile threads of human effort, but with a righteousness that He provides to all who will receive it by faith. With that covering, I can come into His presence with confidence, knowing that I will be received and welcomed.

Not only did this revelation give me boldness in the place of prayer, but for the first time in my life it gave me a sense of security. I had never questioned God's justice; now I would never question His love and mercy. I knew that His mercy extended to even "saved" sinners—that Jesus died for my past, present, and future sins.

Confidence in the place of prayer will increase as you believe that God does not hear your prayers because you are good, but because He is good.

Persistence Pays

The best biblical example of the reward of persistence is found in Matthew 15, where we read of a woman who would not be discouraged by delay:

And behold, a woman of Canaan came from that region and cried unto Him, saying, "Have mercy on me, O Lord, Son of David! My daughter is severely demon-possessed."

But He answered her not a word. And His disciples came and urged Him, saying, "Send her away, for she cries out after us."

But He answered and said, "I was not sent except to the lost sheep of the house of Israel."

Then dame she and worshiped Him, saying, "Lord help me!"

But He answered and said, "It is not good to take the children's bread and throw it to the little dogs."

And she said, "True, Lord, yet even the little dogs eat the crumbs which fall from their masters' table."

Then Jesus answered and said to her, "O woman, great is your faith! Let it be to you as you desire." And her daughter was healed from that very hour (vv. 22-28).

The first thing I notice about this woman is that she was not an Israelite; she was Canaanite, a heathen. Where she got her faith is a mystery. But she knew that Jesus was the Son of David, and that He had the power to help her daughter.

She came pleading, praying, "Lord, have mercy on me. My daughter has a demon in her." The situation was serious. She needed help and she knew where to find it. Notice what these loving disciples said, "Tell her to go away. She is bothering us with her begging."

I am sorry to say, but I have known Christians who have been upset when a fellow-believer prayed with a real burden. Remember, the gravity of the situation will determine the intensity with which we will pray. If the house is burning down with people asleep inside, you do not knock gently on the door and whisper, "Your house is on fire." No, you get excited; you shout out loud and beat on the door. The situation demands it.

This woman had a serious need about which others seemed to have little concern. In fact, her concern bothered them. I remember being in a service one night when a mother wept and cried out to God for her children's salvation. Some were disturbed by her cries. Others tried to calm her. Some did not know what was happening. Paul says, "Rejoice with those who rejoice, and weep with those who weep". (Rom. 12:15) We ought to feel with our brothers and sisters who are under a burden and pray with them.

The disciples simply didn't want to be bothered by this heathen. But notice what Jesus said to them, and I remind you, the woman was right there listening. In her presence He spoke to His disciples these words, "I was sent to help the Jews, the lost sheep of Israel, not the Gentiles." Most of us would have given up seeking help from that source right then, but not this woman. She came up and fell down at His feet. She worshiped Him and cried out, "Lord, help me."

At this point Jesus spoke again, this time to her. "I cannot take the children's bread and throw it to the dogs." Have you ever heard such insulting words? Please believe me when I say that Jesus loves people. He is not a bigot or a racist. He was demonstrating a truth that we need to learn.

When those words came forth I am sure a rustle went through the crowd. Some were no doubt saying, "That's telling the dog." Other were shocked at His words. Then the woman spoke with a humble voice, "Yes, Lord, I am a dog.

I'm not going to argue that point, but even dogs receive the crumbs which fall from their masters' table."

She could have "blown it" at that point, but she had a need and Jesus was her only hope. She had to persist and she did. It was her persistence in the face of disappointment and delay that caused Jesus to say, "O woman, great is you faith."

What lesson can we learn from this woman's experience? I believe we can say: Delay is not necessarily denial.

Not long ago I asked the Lord a direct question: "Lord, when we know the things we are requesting are Your will, why are there, at times, such long delays in the answers?"

Suddenly, in my spirit, I heard this: "The law of relativity operates in the spiritual realm the same as it does in the physical realm."

I knew God was speaking because I would never have had such a thought. I knew little about the law of relativity. God knew that, and He knew just how much I did now about it. As I understood it, this law essentially says that all things in the universe are related. When there is an action, there is a reaction, even if we cannot see it. Nothing happens in a vacuum.

I quickly saw the spiritual lesson. God is not doing only one thing but many things at a time which are related.

When He does something in one place, it affects things in other places. Paul says in Romans 8:28, "All things work together." We hasten so quickly to the "for good" part of the verse that we fail to see a very important truth: Everything is working together.

When I pray, I give God the option of working in the matter that concerns me, but I must realize that because of what He is doing in other places, He may not conform to my time schedule. What He does in answer to my prayer will affect other things He is doing. As the Lord gave me this understanding, I had a mental picture of a large board on which dominos were being set up in intricate designs. Have you seen this happen? When the dominos are all set, someone touches the lead domino and things fall in all directions.

Prayer is something like those dominos. Whenever we pray, we are setting up another domino; someday the Father is going to touch one and things are going to fall into place. So do not grow weary and lose heart; when you are praying according to His will, it will be done.

My father's sister prayed for her two sons until she died, but neither of them was saved. Nevertheless God had heard her prayers. Not long after she went to be with her Lord, her younger son gave his life to Jesus and has been walking with Him many years. The older son resisted the Lord until only a month or so before his death and then he, too, accepted Christ. He joined his praying mother in glory. Praise the Lord!

When you know you are praying the will of God, do not stop. The answer will come. You may not see it, but it will come.

I am fully persuaded that not one unsaved loved one for whose salvation someone has persistently prayed will be lost. That person will be saved. Remember that God is not willing that even one should perish but that all should repent. If we pray, the Spirit will deal with them and they will not be able to resist. They will repent and turn to God.

Persistence in the face of disappointment—maybe that is what it means to be an overcomer. I want to overcome every obstacle and be persistent in the place of prayer. How about you?

CHAPTER FOUR

Praying for Our Needs

For the first twelve years of my pastoral ministry, I preached in churches of a hundred people or less. For months I would go without enough money in my pocket to buy a cup of coffee (not that I drank the stuff then). Despite our financial situation, I never felt deprived. I was learning to trust God for everything, which was difficult at times, but most rewarding—not always in material things, but in developing an understanding of true values. We had a home, not just a house. We always had good transportation and enough to eat. Our clothes were as good or better than those of most of our parishioners.

During the years that followed I watched the healing and miracle ministries that had flourished in the late '40s and '50s wane. Other "faith" ministries developed into a major force, especially in the charismatic community. In my prayer journey I saw many answers, but on one level prayer was increasingly becoming a real mystery to me. I could not understand why God would want me to pray. Could prayer change the mind of God? Was everything predestined? If God had all power and a will about everything, why didn't He just do what he willed? How much power did Satan really have? Could he prevent God from doing what He wanted to do? How did my prayers affect things?

As these questions filled my mind, I wondered if prayer was a waste of time. Yet I kept at it, deciding on occasion to test it out: I would cease to pray for a while and see if it made any discernible difference. In the meantime, I read many books on the subject, and one in particular kept calling me back to the place of prayer. It was E.M. Bounds' 'The Preacher and Prayer'.

In the early '70s I set out to find the answer. With Jesus' promise "Seek and you shall find," I began my search. I carefully studied the prayer that Jesus, the master Teacher, had taught His disciples to pray. I saw it as the perfect pattern and used it in my daily prayers. Though I cannot say that I soon found answers, I felt that following that pattern would lead me to the answers for which I searched. I knew I was on the right track.

In 1977 I received a call to pastor a church in Kilgore, Texas. In a natural sense, this was a step down—from a larger to a smaller church—but believing God was in it, I accepted. While pasturing that church, I began to receive answers to my questions. A missionary, whose name I do not remember, sent me a book titled 'Destined for the Throne' by Paul E. Billheimer. That little book opened the eyes of my understanding and revelation flowed. For eleven years I have received one revelation after another.

New Light on Old Lessons

I previously mentioned the lesson I learned about putting first things first. That may have been the most important thing I learned in those earlier days of my walk with the Lord. Although I had read the words of Jesus recorded in Matthew 6:33 many times, I had somehow failed to see the principle contained therein; "Seek first the kingdom of God and His righteousness, and all these things (the things that you need) shall be added to you."

These words follow two very important statements. First, Jesus said, "Your Father knows the things you have need of before you ask Him" (6-8). Then—after pointing out that the Gentiles (unbelievers) had their attention on material things, such as what they were going to eat and wear—Jesus said, "Your heavenly Father knows that you need all these things" (6:32).

Then in verse 34 comes the linking word "therefore" introducing Jesus' conclusion, "do not worry." Since your Father knows you have need of these things, and since He is a responsible Father, do not worry or be concerned about these things. Your needs will be met simply because you are in the family of God. The Father adopted you. You did not adopt Him. God chose you from among all of the others, as Paul says in Romans 8, and marked you out to be an exact duplicate of His Son.

This being true, we need not plead with God to supply our personal needs; He will do that. We must seek first the kingdom of God and His righteousness; and if we do, Jesus said that 'all' of the things we need will be added unto us.

But someone may ask, How does one seek first the kingdom of God? Jesus had just told His disciples how to do this. If we read carefully what He said, we will learn. In Matthew 6:9, 10 Jesus says, "In this manner therefore, pray....Your kingdom come, Your will be done on earth as it is in heaven." Go before the Lord and pray this prayer; follow this pattern day by day. As you do, not only will His kingdom be established and His will be done in the earth, but in your life also. In addition, every personal need will be met.

I know this sounds simple, and it is, but it is not easy. Why? Because of our natural tendency to be selfish and self-centered. Who wants to pray about some invisible kingdom? When immature Christians pray, they must see immediate, flesh-satisfying results.

Jesus took His closest followers with Him to the place of prayer on the night before His crucifixion. He withdrew from them a little way and prayed in agony of spirit. In a while He returned and found them sleeping. "Could you not watch with Me one hour?" He asked (Matt. 26:40). After the scene had repeated itself three times, Jesus said to them and to us, "The spirit indeed is willing, but the flesh is weak" (v.41). And again He says, "Watch and pray, lest you enter into temptation."

It seems to be the nature of the flesh to be weak where it should be strong, and to be strong where it should be weak. The old, unrenewed nature does not want to pray about matters that do not offer a 'quick fix'. Jesus knew and knows this truth about us so He promised that every need—physical, financial, spiritual and emotional—would be met if we would but seek first the kingdom of God and His righteousness.

I was thoroughly convinced that this principle was true so I taught it to the people of my church. As I did, they practiced it, and some amazing things happened.

Praying Kingdom Prayers

As a church we were praying for Colima, Mexico, a city which at that time had no strong Christian witness. All of our people were praying, "Lord, establish Your kingdom in Colima....Let your will be done there." During this time of concentrated prayer, on of our young married men came home from work to find his wife almost in tears. "Mark, I have had a terrible headache all day. It just won't go away."

In response, Mark put his arms around her and prayed. "Lord, save Colima. Let Your kingdom be established there."

Suddenly, Karen testified later, the headache was gone. It was as if God had given them their own personal witness to the validity of the teaching they had been hearing about putting the kingdom of God first and then trusting God to take care of all their needs.

Not long after that experience, I taught this principle to a small group in East Texas. A young mother there later told me her testimony:

Her eighteen-month-old daughter had been suffering with an eye infection which had stubbornly resisted medical treatment. Shortly after hearing the teaching about putting the kingdom first, she walked through her house and prayed, "Father, establish Your kingdom here in this city, let Your will be done. When that happens, there will be no more infections to trouble our children." A few moments later she looked at her daughter and was utterly amazed to see that the baby's eyes were clear. All the infection was gone. Praise the Lord!

About the same time, Velma and I were in western Kansas conduction a prayer seminar in a Presbyterian church. After I'd taught this principle, a corn farmer came and invited me to visit his farm. The next day we drove out to his house, sitting in the middle of hundreds of acres of mature corn. Every ear was full and hanging down. After I'd seen the lay of the land, that farmer told me his story. He said, "Preacher, it costs forty thousand dollars a year to insure my crop against hail. But when it was time to renew the insurance policy, I felt the Lord telling me that if I put the forty thousand dollars in the missions offering, He would take care of my corn."

I can tell you positively, because I was there, that hail storm had surrounded his property—his neighbors' crops were severely damaged—but no hail had fallen on this man's land. He had put God's kingdom first, and his need had been met.

I do not know if that man ever had the Lord challenge him in that way again, and I am not suggesting that everyone should drop insurance, but if the Lord tells you to, do it. He 'will' keep His word; the key is to put God first.

Not long afterward I was given my own personal proof that the kingdom-first principle is valid. Our youngest daughter, Terri, had been a diabetic since she was seven years of age. Her doctor told her that if she intended to have children she should do so while she was young. When she and her husband decided that they did in fact want a child, she became pregnant. She soon noticed a problem with one of her eyes and saw an ophthalmologist. His examination showed that blood vessels behind the retina of her eye were bursting. He said she would require laser treatments, but when he found out she was pregnant, he implied that unless she terminated the pregnancy she might go blind. He sent her to her gynecologist, who sent her to a specialist, who told her that if she didn't terminate the pregnancy she might not live more than five years. His prognosis was that what was happening in the eyes would probably happen in her kidneys. He saw an abortion as her only alternative.

Velma was with Terri when she received this news, and Velma came home in tears. When I heard the story, I immediately went before the Lord. "Father, have mercy on us," I pleaded. But I knew I was facing my own personal test of the kingdom-first principle that I taught so fervently. I said, "Father, I have been teaching that if we seek first Your kingdom and righteousness, You will take care of matters such as this. "I continued, "Lord, if what I have been teaching is right, that doctor is going to do a 180-degree turn in his prognosis. If he doesn't change, I will assume that what I have taught is not the truth, and I will never teach it again."

Well, Terri and her husband decided to proceed and scheduled the operation for the following Thursday. Velma and I just kept praying. "Your kingdom come, Your will be done." On Tuesday, before the scheduled abortion, the doctor called my daughter to his office for further consultation. When she got there, he had done a 180-degree turn. On the basis of a number of articles he'd read the night before, he recommended an alternative treatment that he thought would be safe for her and the baby.

Michelle was born on April 18, 1900. She knows she would not be here if Jesus had not intervened. And I know that the kingdom-first principle is true—and it works.

Solomon's Example

First Kings 3 records an interesting event in the life of Solomon. Shortly after he became king of Israel, God spoke to him in a dream: "Ask! What shall I give you?" (v. 5). The Lord was telling Solomon, "Ask for anything you desire and it will be given to you."

Solomon responded by confessing his weakness and inability to rule: "I am a little child; I do not know how to go out or come in" (v. 7). He asked for wisdom and discernment to rule the nation of Israel justly: "Give to Your servant an understanding heart to judge Your people"(v. 9). The Lord was pleased with Solomon's request and replied that He would give Solomon wealth and honor in addition to wisdom: "Because you have asked this thing, and 'have not asked...for yourself...I have also given you what you have not asked" (v. 11, italics added).

Isn't it interesting that God would say to Solomon, " Because you did not ask, I am going to give you wealth and honor in addition to the thing you requested"? This illustrates the very principle Jesus taught His disciples in Matthew 6:33.

I cannot tell you the scores of people who have been set free by this simple truth. Jesus is not saying we should never ask for personal things. He is saying that the kingdom must be first. With this in mind we can pray with a much greater sense of expectancy.

Chapter Five

Unrealistic Expectations

One of the most puzzling problems faced by many Bible-believing Christians is reconciling the seemingly limitless positive promises of the Word with the limitations of those promises in their experience.

We read the Scriptures (which we are told mean what they say); we do what they say, and nothing happens. "Call to Me, and I will answer you, and show you great and mighty things, which you do not know" (Jer. 33:3); "Whatever things you ask when you pray, believe that you receive them, and you will have them" (Mark 11:24); "If two of you agree on earth concerning anything that they ask, it will be done for them by My Father in heaven" (Matt. 18:19).

These promises seem to be unlimited. They seem to say anyone can ask anything, anytime, and it will be done. This, however, does not appear to be the case with many who pray. They ask very sincerely, believing that God can do what they ask, but nothing happens. Why doesn't God do what He has said He would do? These promises seem to cover every need; physical, financial, spiritual, and emotional. But do they really? Are there qualifications and/or limitations that are not stated? Recognizing that I am treading on "holy ground," I am choosing my words very deliberately. After many years of walking with the Lord, I have become convinced that every promise of God has limitations, either stated or implied.

Are the Promises Limited?

When we speak we expect those who hear to understand the things we say at the present moment in the context of what we have said in the past. That is why we must read 'all' God's Word. All of God's promises have a relevant background; we cannot lift a promise out of its setting and try to stand on it. To do so can be very disappointing. Some apparently unlimited promises have limitations; to be properly understood they must be examined in the context of the entire revelation of God in His Word. God will not do for me those things which are contrary to His loving nature. He will not do anything that would cause Him to violate His holy character. he will do nothing that is wrong. He does not answer the prayers of rebels and the willfully disobedient, unless those prayers are for forgiveness. He will not answer those who are selfish and self-centered. God will not do for us what He told us to do; that is, we cannot delegate to God what He delegated to us. Do you see? "Whosoever" does not apply to everyone. "Anything" does not mean "everything."

As Jesus often said, "If you have ears to hear, hear." The truth will not destroy you faith; it will make you free (see John 8:32). Doubt, frustration, unbelief, anger and depression often are the result of having only a part of the truth.

Let me illustrate; Let's suppose I worked for a rancher; I'd been working for this man for many years, and I trusted him completely. He had never told me anything but the truth.; he always kept his word. One day he says to me, "Bob, I want you to build a fence from the southwest corner of my property to the northwest corner." I load the posts, the wire and the tools necessary to do the job onto the pickup truck. As I am about to drive away, the rancher says, "If you need anything, give me a call on the CB and I'll get it out to you as soon as I can."

As I work, I get to thinking about what the boss said. He said, "If you need 'anything', give me a call." I remind myself of the boss's honesty and integrity. This man would not lie. He said "anything," and if he said it, he meant it.

So I decide to give him a call. "Boss, do you remember telling me that if I needed anything I could give you a call?"

"Yes, I sure do. What do you need?"

To test him I reply, "You did say 'anything'. didn't you?"

"Yes," he responds, "what do you need?"

"Well, I need a new car...."

Now, do you think the rancher's "anything" applied to a new car? Of course not. Though it was not clearly stated, the 'anything' applied only to things having to do with building the fence.

God's 'anything' has the same implied limitations. He is saying, "Anything that will help you do what I have sent you to do will be granted." In that context God will supply as quickly as He can. He is not just building fences; He is building fence-builders. He is more concerned about us that about what we are doing. He is more interested in working in us than through us. He is working in us both to will and to do His good pleasure" Phil 2:13, KJV).

We must pray: "Lord, Your will and Your kingdom are the most important things. Help me do what you have told me to do. Equip me with the tools to build the things You have put in my heart to build." Whatever I need to do the work He commanded me to do will be supplied. Yet those things may not come until we have expended all of our personal resources. When we have come to our end, God begins.

Paul said, "My God shall supply all your need according to His riches in glory by Christ Jesus" (Phil. 4:19). It does not say all wants and desires will be supplied---only needs.

Many of our expectations are not realistic because they are built on false assumptions. False assumptions produce false hope, and as Solomon said, "Hope deferred makes the heart sick' (Prov. 13:12. God has not promised to be all things to all men. he has not committed Himself to doing anything and everything we ask.

Praying in Jesus' Name

This teaching is right in line with Jesus' words: "Whatever you ask in My name, that I will do, that the Father may be glorified in the son. If you ask anything in My name, I will do it" (John 14:13,14). What a powerful, seemingly all-inclusive verse of Scripture, but the qualifying clause is "ask in My name."

I was considering this promise one day while praying, and I recalled various teachings on the passage that I had either heard or read. One brother had said, "It is as though Jesus has given us a blank check on the bank of heaven and has instructed us to fill it out in any amount and present it to be cashed." Well, I had done that and my checks had bounced.

Another had said, "Jesus has given us 'power of attorney'; we have the authority to use His name to get what we need."

Suddenly I said out loud, "Lord, that does not work. I've asked things in Jesus' name and they have not been done.

I had no sooner spoken when the Father said, "Son, you do not know what it means to ask in Jesus' name." As I thought about that word, I knew He was right. I did not know how to ask in Jesus' name. All I was doing was presenting my 'want list' and then saying, "In Jesus' name, amen." It seemed to me that I was using that name without any real understanding of what it meant.

The Lord did not give any further explanation, so I got down my interlinear Greek New Testament and Thayer's Greek-English Lexicon and searched for understanding. To my surprise, a thorough study revealed that—if expanded to its fullest meaning in English—Jesus was in effect saying, "Whatever you ask by My command and authority, acting in My behalf, for the advancement of My kingdom, I will do, that the Father may be glorified in the Son."

To pray in Jesus' name took on a new meaning. Suddenly, the kingdom comes back into focus. Prayer was to be primarily in behalf of His kingdom. I could see it. We have been authorized to act in his behalf for the advancement of His kingdom.

When one is deputized by the sheriff of a given county, he is given power (gun) and authority (badge). All deputies know that they have no authority to act in their own behalf. They may not impose their will on others except according to the laws of the county. They must act in behalf of the one who gave them their authority.

Our king has given us authority but not to act in our own behalf. We act in His behalf. We may not use the power given to us to satisfy our selfish desires, not even our needs.

Jesus' Example

After Jesus was baptized by John in the River Jordan, He was led by the Spirit into the wilderness to be tested by Satan (see Matt. 4:1). Forty days Jesus spent in the wilderness of Judea with food. At the end of those days He was hungry. While Jesus was in this weakened condition, Satan came to Him and said, "Since You are the Son of God, command that these stones become bread" (4:3, author's paraphrase). Jesus certainly had the power to do what Satan suggested. He could have used His power to fulfill His own personal need, but He refused to do so. To Satan He said, "Man shall not live by bread alone, but by every word that proceeds from the mouth of God" (4:4).

Shortly before His ascension, Jesus called His disciples around Him and told the, "As the Father has sent me, I also send you"—in the very same manner, with the very same authority (John 20:21). Then, as He breathed upon the, He said, "Receive the Holy Spirit" (John 20:22). (I personally believe they were immediately 'born again'; life from above flowed into the.) A few days later they received the power of Jesus. When they did, they went out to do His will, not their own.

It may seem that I am overemphasizing the point, but if prayer is to be a meaningful experience, the pray-er must understand that we are in this world to act in behalf of the one who called us. If prayer is to be truly effectual, it must be unselfish. James, our Lord' brother, said, "You ask and receive not because you ask out of wrong motives, that you may satisfy your own selfish desires" (James 4:3, author's paraphrase)—which leads me to another important lesson in prayer.

Chapter Six

The Idolatry of Self-Centeredness

I was in my prayer closet one morning meditating on the Lord and His Word when He spoke to me. In my spirit I heard Him say, "Son, all sin is idolatry." I was sure I had either heard or read that statement before, so I said, "Lord, I think I have heard that, but I do not understand it."

He answered, "All sin is a manifestation of selfishness and self-centeredness, and this is idolatry."

As I thought about it, I could see that this was true. Pride was the manifestation of selfishness that caused Lucifer to fall from his exalted place by the throne of God. Satan in turn tempted Eve with self-worship: "You will be like God" (see Gen. 3:3-5). She was enticed and deceived. Believing Satan's lie, her desire to be independent caused her and her husband to eat of the tree.

The root of lust also is selfishness. Hate, unforgiveness, greed, avarice, jealousy, fear—all are but manifestations of selfishness. I, me, mine and my are among the most often-used words in the vocabulary of the average person.

It is tragic, but we may be living in the most self-centered generation ever produced. We seem to face every new possibility with the question, What am I going to get out of it? So often new relationships are developed with ulterior motives. We say to ourselves, This person may be able to help me reach my goals; I can use him or her. Or we might say, I can't see how this person can help me, so I'm not going to go out of my way to develop a meaningful relationship. This does not put us in a very good light, but I fear it is the truth.

One of the great tragedies of our times is that just such a spirit has gotten into the church. Much of the teaching in the church and on TV in recent years has strengthened the desires of the flesh and generated a lust for material things. Please do not hear these words as a blanket indictment of every positive ministry on TV and in the church—it is not. But when carnal Christians hear a message on making a positive confession and getting the desires of one's heart—a message that says God wants all of His people to be prosperous materially and His special favor will come upon anyone who believes—carnal Christians will do what they are told will release the blessing of God upon their lives.

They give to get, and what they get they consume upon their own lusts. Unfortunately, there are charlatans who prey upon this human weakness for their own selfish purposes. David warns, "If riches increase, do not set your heart on them" (Ps. 62:10). Paul writes of material riches only once, saying they are 'uncertain' (see 1 Tim. 6:17). People who receive a steady diet of this king of teaching will pray self-centered, self –serving prayers. If selfishness is idolatry, we must repent and ask God to forgive us.

Selflessness Needed

Selfishness—being concerned excessively or exclusively with oneself—is the natural tendency of the flesh. We will never be totally free from it in this life, but with understanding and the help of the Holy Spirit we can be less selfish.

Selflessness must be one of the most important goals of our lives. Jesus is our example. He said to His followers, "If anyone desires to come after Me, let him deny himself, and take up his cross, and follow me" (Matt. 16:24). He did not lead His followers to a throne; He led them to a cross. He did not lead them to wealth but to self-denial. He did not lead them to fame but to indignity. Not to victory, but to what seemed to be defeat. One cannot experience resurrection until there has been a crucifixion—a crucifixion of the self-life.

In Ephesians 4:12,13 Paul reveals that God's intention is the perfecting and the full equipping of the saints that we might develop until we all attain oneness in the faith and in the comprehension of the full and accurate knowledge of the Son of God, in order that we might arrive at mature adulthood—the completeness of personality which is nothing less than Christ's own perfection. This implies spiritual progression—a growth toward maturity.

One of the greatest joys of parents is to see their children grow up. I will never forget the day our first daughter, Vicky, did a totally unselfish thing. She was about eight years old and was going to town with her grandmother. He mother gave her twenty-five cents to spend. When she returned home she had bought several presents: a bread dish for her mother, purchased at a rummage sale for five cents, and a gift for each of her two sisters with the remaining twenty cents. When her mother questioned her, "What did you buy for yourself?" she replied, "I didn't need anything. They were giving away balloons and I got one of them." We were so proud of her that day, and she is still one of the most unselfish people I know.

Victory Over Fear

In the early years of my Christian walk and ministry, I learned by personal experience how devastating self-centeredness and selfishness can be. It was in my first church. As if inexperience and little training were not enough, I was suffering from extreme fear. Fear of death, fear of failing, fear of sickness dominated my thoughts. I was a hypochondriac with an extreme case of claustrophobia.

It was almost impossible for me to visit hospitals. The smell of them made me sick, and in spite of my prayers and the prayers of others, the conditions prevailed. I prayed for others and they were helped, but nothing seemed to help me.

This was the state of things the morning Bud Tillman knocked on my door. There he stood, trembling all over, on the verge of a total nervous collapse. I invited him in and asked him to sit down. His first words were, "Nine of my dad's people have committed suicide, and I know that is what is going to happen to me." There it was, out in the open.

He had needed to say this to someone for a long time and I think he felt a little relief, but he needed something more. Not knowing exactly what to say, I said, "Bud, let's pray." I knew we could not go wrong in praying.

Not more than five minutes had passed when I suddenly knew what to say and how to say it. What I was to say and the tone of voice in which I was told to say it were totally contrary to my temperament. I have my mother's temperament—I never want to hurt anyone and will do anything to avoid it. But what I was hearing from God was going to hurt.

I stopped praying, turned to Bud and said, "Bud, you are the most self-centered person I have ever met. He you are, telling me you might commit suicide, and if you did we would not miss you two weeks. You are a Christian, but you are not concerned about anyone but yourself. People are dying and going to hell, but do you care? No, you just pray over your own problems."

His neck and face turned red. He had certainly not expected to hear his pastor say such unkind words. He was no longer worried about killing himself; he was thinking about killing me. I had changed his fear to anger.

I didn't know what I was doing, but God did. Later, Bud told me that, as he cooled down, he realized that I had spoken the truth. he adjusted his thinking, eventually married, had a family and is still living. His testimony was, "I never had anything help me as much in all my life." All I had said was "You are selfish and self-centered." His response to that revelation made the difference.

Well, Bud was not even out of sight when God spoke these words: "That is what is the matter with you, too."

I was shocked. Me? selfish and self-centered? I thought I was unselfish. I had denied myself the security of a place in my father's manufacturing plant to go into the ministry—where at times we had almost nothing. I had always been a giver. I would share anything and everything I had with others.

Then I heard in my spirit, "This inordinate fear is a manifestation of selfishness and self-centeredness."

Suddenly I knew I had the answer. At the root of fear was sin. All I had to do was confess the sin of selfishness and self-centeredness and change my way of thinking. This I did, and I began to walk in the light of that revelation. My fears subsided. In a short time I was walking in the full peace of God.

Now, after many years of ministering to those having emotional and marital problems, I am convinced that at the root of most of those problems is the sin of selfishness.

Many people deal with only the fruit—not the root—of their depression, jealousy, lust, greed, pride or bitterness. When you see that the root of the problem is sin, you can experience tremendous help. Kill the root and you will eliminate the fruit. Pick the fruit and it will come back again. I hope you are not asking, "What does all of this have to do with prayer?" if you are? Let me explain: You will never be truly effective in prayer until you learn to deal with this sin of selfishness--which is nothing more than idolatry.

CHAPTER SEVEN

How Can We Know the Will of God?

Another question often asked by sincere Christians is, How can I know the will of God? Some seem almost paranoid about possibly missing God's will. I've heard people say, "I think God is trying to tell me something." My response to that statement is: "God is not 'trying ' to do anything. If He wants to tell you something, He will." We are inclined to think of God in human terms, as if He were a man—only bigger and more powerful. No so, "As the heavens are higher than the earth, so are My ways higher than your ways, and My thoughts than your thoughts" (Is. 55:9).

It is important to know His will, though it is not absolutely essential. But we can pray most effectively when we know just exactly what God's will is in a matter. Paul admonished the church at Ephesus, "Do not be unwise, but understand what the will of the Lord is" (5:17).

In I John 5:14,15 we read: "This is the confidence that we have in Him, that if we ask anything according to His will, He hears us. And if we know that He hears us...we know that we have the petitions that we have asked of Him." The qualifying phrase here is "according to His will." The promise is that we will receive an answer to our petition. If we know His will, we can pray with greater faith. But you may ask, "How can I be sure that I know His will?"

Revelation

One way that we can know God's will is by direct revelation. That is, He may speak a 'rhema' word to us—anyone of us, mature or immature, educated or uneducated. Peter received such a work. Matthew 16:13-17 records that Jesus asked His disciples, "Who do men say that I, the Son of Man, am?" Their reply was, "Some say John the Baptist, some Elijah, others Jeremiah or one of the prophets." Then Jesus asked, "But who do you say that I am?" Immediately Peter answered, "You are the Christ, the Son of the Living God."

I think Peter surprised himself. He was not sure how he knew it, but out came those words: "You are the Christ." Jesus responded, "Blessed are you...for flesh and blood has not revealed this to you, but My Father who is in heaven." In effect Jesus was saying, "Peter you have received a revelation. It came from God and was not based in logic or reason." Peter could not have explained how he knew who Jesus was, but he did. Many of us have had just such an experience. We know, but we don't know how we know. By an inner witness we know and can say, "You are the Christ."

There are times when God speaks in such clear tones that we think our ears heard something. Though I have never to my knowledge heard the audible voice of God, I have heard Him speak in my spirit many times. he speaks through inner impressions. He speaks through circumstances. He speaks through others. He speaks through His Word. If He is speaking to you, you will know it. His sheep know His voice. There is no doubt about it.

I have heard testimonies of people who while living in deep sin heard the voice of God so clearly that they knew who it was. A former atheist once told me that while she was far away from God He spoke to her and told her He loved her just as she was. She was so overwhelmed by His voice that she followed Him from that very day.

God does not lead His people today by a pillar of fire and a cloud. He has given us His Spirit to live within us and to guide us in the ways He would have us go. You may not see anything or hear anything, but you can know that God has spoken. In you "knower", in your deepest being, you intuitively know that God has spoken and that you perceive His will in a matter. When this happens you may say, "I do not know how I know, but I do know that God wants me to do this—or not do that.

There is a level of spiritual maturity where you know His will because you have been walking so closely in His presence. You have heard His voice so often that you know what to do when the time comes, even if you do not hear anything at the moment.

A member of a church I was pasturing in Arkansas came to me one day and said, "Pastor, I'm getting ready to make a million dollars." He had just received a rather large insurance settlement which he then invested in the commodities market—pork bellies, as I remember it. He was excited because he had made thirty thousand dollars in a couple of days. He was certain that within a few days he would be a millionaire.

Within a few days he was back in my office, no longer excited. He was 'locked' in the market and could not get out; it was costing him a lot of money. Of course he wanted prayer. After we prayed together, I said, "I believe you will be able to get out next Friday."

I had not heard a voice. I had not seen a vision. I just knew in my "knower" that come Friday he could get out of the market without a loss. On Tuesday, when there was a little movement in the market, my friend got out, but not without a great loss. Later we found out that if he had waited until Friday he could have gotten out of the market without a loss.

Some people might call such a thing a 'holy hunch' ; I call it "knowing in your spirit." In his book 'The Spiritual Man', Watchman Nee says that one of the functions of the human spirit is to "know things intuitively." When the human spirit is alive and filled with the Spirit of God, it functions the way it was designed to function. And when the human spirit is functioning the way it was designed to function, it will hear the voice of God. It will know the will of the Father.

Jesus had a spirit that functioned properly—He always knew the will of the Father. "But," I hear someone object, "He was the Son of God—He had inside information." It is true, He was the Son of God. But we who have been born from above are also, "children of God" (see I John 3:2). And we have a reborn spirit that has the potential to hear God and to know the will of our Father: "As many as are led by the Spirit of God, these are the sons of God" (Rom. 8:14).

We have the same access to the Father that Jesus had as a man. Jesus was living as any other human being while He was here on earth. To know the will of His Father He had to spend quality time with Him. The same is true of us.

This leads me to the second way we come to know His will-through relationship. To know God's will truly, we need to know Him. When we really know Him, we know His will.

Relationship

Knowing God is the highest pursuit in which a human can be involved. The apostle Paul had experienced great hardship in his pursuit of knowing God, yet in his letter to the Philippians he still expressed this as the deepest desire of his heart: "That I may know Him and the power of His resurrection, and the fellowship of His sufferings" (3:10). Paul was saying, "I want to know Him as intimately and completely as I know He can be known." Then in Colossians 1:9 Paul said that he prays diligently for other Christians to be "filled with the knowledge of His will in all wisdom and spiritual understanding."

My desire for you is that you may get to know Him—to know Him as intimately as I know He can be known. When you know Him you will know His will. And when you know Him and His will, you will align your will with His will and pray on earth what God wills in heaven.

How do we get to know Him? Exactly as we would get to know anyone. We must spend quality time with Him—in prayer. If you can do that over a period of years you will know His nature and His character. And when you know

His nature and His character, you will be able to look at a given situation and know God's will. You will know that He never acts contrary to His nature or out of character.

Listen to people talk about the things of God and you will discern very quickly what they know of the nature and character of God. Listen to them read the Bible, and you can hear by the tone they give to the voice of God just how well they know Him.

For many years now, I have read the Bible with no other purpose in mind than to know God as He is revealed in His holy Word. I have long since given up trying to prop up my doctrines with Scripture verses scattered here and there. A long time ago I found that you can prove just about anything with the Word of God if you are subtle enough. My understanding of God and my knowledge of Him have come from spending quality time in His presence, listening to what He says. I do not come into His presence to have Him agree with me. I come to agree with Him. he is always right. And as I meditate on His Word, I begin to know His nature and His character. his Word tells me what He has done, what He is going to do, and how He has dealt with different situations in the lives of His people. As I learn, I am corrected and encouraged, changed into his image. Hallelujah!

I am not reading His Word to find out when Jesus is coming back. I am discovering, through His truth, that He is already here. Jesus could not be more real if He were to manifest Himself in the flesh. How can I say such a thing? Well, Paul says we don't know Christ according to the flesh (see 2 Cor. 5:16)—we know our Lord through the Spirit. If He were here in His physical body, He would be confined to a specific place; I could live across the world from Him and never see Him. But through the indwelling Spirit I can have a continuous, living relationship with my Lord. He is real, as real as life itself. Jesus said to His disciples, "It is to your advantage that I go away..." (John 16:7). I believe what He said. Yes, I believe He is returning to this earth in bodily form—and this refers to the body He left in, not the church. In Acts 1:11, right after our Lord's ascension, and angel told the disciples, "This same Jesus...will so come in like manner as you saw Him go into heaven."

What is God Like?

Let's take a closer look at who God is. Here is what the apostle John has to say. "Beloved, let us love one another, for love is of God; and everyone who loves is born of God and knows God. He who does not love does not know God, for 'God is love" (I John 4:7,8, italics added).

In His true essence, the unchanging God is love. Therefore, He is compassionate, merciful, patient, forgiving—not willing that even one should perish. He does not have to try to be merciful. To be unmerciful would be contrary to His nature. It is not a effort for Him to be patient. Because He is love, He is patient. God is not patient just on the days He feels good. He does not forgive because He is in a forgiving mood. It is His nature. He cannot be love and be unkind. Unforgiveness is contrary to His nature. Man's conduct cannot change the nature of God. He does not change. We have His own word on the matter.

The English word 'love' is used often in the New Testament in reference to God: in the Greek the noun is 'agape'; the verb is 'agapeo'. 'Agape' is what God is; 'agapeo' is what He does to show us who He is. Unlike us, God loves the unlovely. He loves us when we were sinners, when we were living in willful disobedience and rebellion: "But God demonstrates His own love toward us, in that while we were still sinners, Christ died for us" (Rom. 5:8). His love is not limited to a few select ones: "For God so loved the world that He gave His only begotten Son, that whoever believes in Him should not perish but have everlasting life" (John 3:16).

What was the 'good news' of the gospel? It can be stated in a few words: God is love. Until Jesus came, the world had little understanding of what God was really like. God had revealed His holy character, but only a few was His loving nature. The Old Testament reveals His character. The New

Testament reveals His nature. his nature is love; His character is holy. This distinction is very important.

In the Word, God is called the Holy One or the Holy One of Israel forty-seven times. In Revelations, one of the seven angels declares, "You are righteous, O Lord" (16:5). God Himself said, "I the Lord your God am holy" (Lev. 19:2). These words, 'holy' and 'righteous', are adjectives used to describe an attribute of God. This God who is love in His true essence and nature is holy in character. His holy character requires Him to do right. Not what you or I think is right, but what 'is' right. He always knows and always does right.

Like Paul, I do not know Him as well as I want to know Him. That is why I set aside time daily to be in His presence. if others seem to know Him better than you do, it may be that they are spending more time with Him.

Jesus always knew His father's will because He spent time alone with Him in the place of prayer. That is why He could say, "The Son can do nothing of Himself, but what He sees the Father do" (John 5:19); "I do not seek my own will but the will of the Father who sent me" (John 5:30); "The words that I speak to you I do not speak on My own authority; but the Father who dwells in Me does the works" (John 14:10). Jesus was totally submissive to the Father; He had no will of His own. Isn't that where we want to be in our spiritual walk?

Jesus Knew God's Will

It is clear that Jesus did the Father's will, but how could He always be sure of what His Father willed?

The answer can be seen in the record of His walk on earth. mark reports, "Having risen a long while before daylight, He went out and departed to a solitary place; and there He prayed" (1:35). Matthew tells us that after Jesus left the multitude, "He went up on a mountain by Himself to pray" (Matt. 14:23). He was always going to or coming from the place of prayer. At times He spent all night praying.

Jesus was so in tune with His Father that He could know: When I heal someone, I am doing exactly what My Father has told Me to do. When I raise someone from the dead, I am doing exactly what My Father has told me to do. When I cast out demons, I am doing exactly what My Father has told Me to do.

Jesus did not even attempt to do anything unless His Father was telling Him to do it. Sometimes He healed every person in a place. Other times He healed only one among a multitude. He stopped a few funeral processions in His lifetime and raised people to life again, but not all. He did just what His Father told Him to do, no more and no less. And remember, to His disciples He said, "As the Father has sent Me, I also send you" (John 20:21). It is evident from these words that we are in the world not to do our will but the will of Him who sent us.

Spending Time

If we are here in this world to do His will, it is best that we know His will. how are we going to know His will if we do not spend quality time in His presence? And how will we hear His voice, if we do all the talking? We must be listeners when we come into His presence.

Knowing the will of God is simple but not easy. It is simple because it requires nothing more than spending quality time in the presence of Him whose will you seek to know. That's all. But that is not easy, because of the demands of the flesh. The flesh wants to 'do' something, go into action. To the flesh, prayer is a passive endeavor. But the truth of the matter is that nothing we do will make any real difference unless it is motivated by the Holy Spirit. For a work to be a work of God, it must be conceived through the Spirit in the place of prayer. It must be carried out in the energy of the Spirit.

Anything else, regardless of how it may appear, is a work of the flesh. It may be a good work, but good works of the flesh are not acceptable to God, who does not see things as we see them. This is the reason the Scriptures warn that many who are first here will be last in the presence of God. He knows which works are of Him and which are of the flesh. We may call some works good; He may call them bad. We may call some spiritual; He may call them carnal. Remember, His ways are higher than ours.

It seems the disciples followed the example the Lord set before them. Acts I says that after the Lord's ascension about 120 of His followers went back into Jerusalem and continued in prayer.

Acts 2 records that as they prayed the Holy Spirit was poured out upon them, miraculous manifestations of His presence were experienced by the disciples. These manifestations were so unusual that a multitude of people—many from other nations—came together to see what was going on. Many foreigners were astonished when they heard these Galileans speaking their native languages, some thought they were drunk with wine. But as a result of Peter's preaching Jesus, three thousand souls repented and received baptism. Then we read in verse 42: "They continued steadfastly in the apostles' doctrine and fellowship, in the breaking of bread, and in prayers." Somehow those new converts knew they were to pray. And as they prayed the Lord kept adding to the church daily those who were being saved.

In Acts 3 we see Peter and John going to the temple at the time of prayer. On their way to the prayer meeting, a paralytic beggar asked them for some money. Peter said, "I don't have money, but I do have something you need more that money. In the name of Jesus Christ of Nazareth, rise up and walk". The power of God went through that poor man and suddenly he was running through the temple, walking and leaping and praising God (see vv. 1:10).

This story illustrates just how important it is to know the will of God. We can do only the things He has authorized. it is quite possible that Jesus Himself had passed by this beggar previously. Scripture says the man was past forty years of age and that he was laid daily at the temple gate called Beautiful in Jerusalem. Jesus came into Jerusalem through that gate and had not ministered to this man. Why? Jesus did only what His Father told Him to do. There were times when Jesus healed everyone present in a place; other times He healed only a few.

For some time, Peter and John had been going up to the temple to pray, day after day, yet they had not ministered to this man. But on this day, Peter had the authority to do what he did. Obviously the Lord had spoken to him. There is no reason to believe that Peter had greater faith that day than the day before, nor is there any evidence to sustain the view that the beggar had greater faith that day. Peter did not have a sudden burst of internal energy which made it possible for him to minister successfully to this poor man. What was different about that day? I believe that Peter then received the authority to minister healing to this man. Peter was so in tune with God that he knew what to do.

Is such a relationship possible now? Yes! It is possible, but it is not easy because of the weakness of the flesh. however, if we do not believe that such a relationship is possible, we will never try to enter into it. James says, "Draw near to God and He will draw near to you" (4:8). Moses put it another way: "You will find Him is you seek Him with all your heart and with all your soul" (Deut. 4:29).

Diligence is required. The whole heart and soul must seek Him. And the seeking must be directed toward His face and not His hand. Far too many of us are so interested in His hand and what we hope to receive from it that we never seek His face. If you want to see His hand, seek His face. Seek His hand only, and you will see neither His hand nor His face.

Paul was not seeking anything from God; he simply wanted to know Him. That would be enough. Anything that God would do for Paul was insignificant compared to knowing Him. And Paul knew that to know Him would require more than giving God a few minutes of time when he could fit it into his busy schedule. Knowing God was a priority. And if we are to know Him, we must be prepared to give Him the best hour of our day.

I've read that John Wesley's mother spent two hours each day in communication with her Lord—in spite of the fact that she had fifteen children to care for. She wanted to know Him, and she knew it would take time, quality time, in His presence.

After fifty years in the school of prayer, I believe I can speak from the wisdom of experience. Early morning is the time for prayer. Jesus arose long before daylight and went to prayer (see Mark 1:35). I have found that if I do not begin the day with prayer, I often end it the way it began. The mind is fresh in the morning; the body is renewed and rested. the first hour is the best hour and I have determined to give my best to God. David says in Psalm 5:3: "My voice you shall hear in the morning, O Lord; in the morning I will direct it (my prayer) to You, and I will look up."

Someone may be saying, "I just can't get up in the morning. I'm a night person." My question to you is: "Are you a house of prayer?" If you are, no problem; continue the way you are. Whether you have established time in the morning or at night, keep your schedule with God.

In the early church there were set hours of prayer. Acts 3:1 tells us that one of those hours was 3:00 p.m. Some believe that early Christians followed the patterns of the Jews in prayer: they prayed at 6:00 a.m., 3:00 p.m. and 9:00 p.m. From the evidence presented in the book of Acts, they prayed at other times as well. If one read Acts 3 carefully, one can see that the early church had a set time and an established place for daily prayer.

Study the lives of the Old Testament saints. You will find that they spent much time seeking God. David said, "As the deer pants for the water brooks, so pants my soul for You, O God. My soul thirsts for God, for the living God" (Ps. 42:1,2. Isaiah cried out, "With my soul I have desired You in the night; yes, by my spirit within me I will seek You early" (Is. 26:9).

When we seek Him with that kind of diligence, we will know Him—and we will know His will. When we know His will, we can pray intelligently about a matter. When we pray intelligently about a matter, there will be an answer every time. When we enter into this dimension, we no longer pray and hope; we pray and expect the answer to come. Some may say that it is not possible to enter into this kind of relationship with God, that we cannot hope always to know the will of God. My response is that Jesus did. Jesus always knew His Father's will, and if He did, we can.

We 'can' spend the time necessary to know God. The question is: Will we? Will you take the time required to know God?

These are times that require extraordinary prayers—prayers that come from those who know God; those who have an intimate relationship with Him; those who want the will of God more than their own; those who will pray without ceasing, knowing that God will hear and answer.

Chapter Eight

Why Pray?

Why would an omnipotent, omniscient God need us to pray? Can He not do what He wants to do without us? Is there something God lacks that we can contribute to Him, some insufficiency that we can supply through our prayer? Several years ago I began to ask these questions. Frankly, I could not find answers. I read most of the classics on prayer and found that they said almost the same things. They discussed different kinds of prayer, including the how-to of prayer, but none seemed to go into the why of prayer.

As I analyzed my own prayers, I saw that most of what I was calling prayer was not prayer at all. As I listened to myself and others pray, I realized that one would get the impression that God didn't know very much. Prayer seemed to be an informing session, where I told God about things that perhaps He had overlooked. Sometimes prayer was an instructing session, where I would tell God how He should deal with certain matters. It was as though He would not know just what to do unless He had my suggestions or directions. At other times I heard myself praying as if God were not as concerned about a matter as He should be. It was my duty to stir Him up somehow to where His concern would equal mine. As these patterns became obvious, I realized that much of my prayer time was an exercise in futility.

God Created

To understand the purpose of prayer you must know how God implements His will in this universe, and to understand that we must go back to the beginning.

"In the beginning God created the heavens and the earth" (Gen. 1:1). Paul tells us: "By Him (Jesus) all things were created that are in heaven and that are on earth, visible and invisible, whether thrones or dominions or principalities or powers. All things were created through Him and for Him. And He is before all things, and in Him all things consist" (Col. 1:16,17). Every part of the creation was created in perfect order and balance, sustained and held together by Christ. God did not create the fish before He created the water. First grass was created, then the cattle. God built into His creation an amazing interdependence. All living things depend upon other living things, and the whole community of living things has a corporate dependence on the environment.

The universe God created was designed to function under a system of law: natural, physical laws and spiritual laws. Those who study such matters tell us there are multiplied billions of systems like our own Milky Way, each with its billions of stars orbiting around the center of the universe. And every planet revolves around its sun and is held in its place—by law. Our God created it all and He Himself operates within the laws He established. He does not change the length of the days. He does not make a decision about weather. Those things are determined by law. When warm, moisture-laden air meets a cool front, clouds will form and precipitation will fall. Nothing supernatural about it. That is the law. And God Himself does not supersede those laws unless it can be done legally.

Up until the sixth creative day all was well and good. But on the sixth day, God created a potential problem:

Then God said, "Let Us make man in Our image, according to Our likeness; let them have dominion over the fish of the sea, over the birds of the air, and over the cattle, over all the earth and over every creeping thing that creeps on the earth." So God created man in His own image; in the image of God He created him; male and female He created them. Then God blessed them, and God said to them, "Be fruitful and multiply; fill the earth and subdue it; have dominion over the fish of the sea, over the birds of the air, and over every living thing that moves on the earth" (Gen. 1:26-28).

When God created man and woman and placed them upon the earth, He gave them dominion over every living thing. Though we do not find anywhere in the Word that man was given 'free will', we believe that he was because of the way God dealt with him. Genesis 2:16 shows that Adam was given the right to decide whether or not he would obey God's command. He was not forced to obey or to disobey. The choice was his, though he was told the price of disobedience. Genesis 3:1-6 tells the story of the decision that was made and how Adam and Eve disobeyed God.

Adam's decision did not catch God off guard. He who knows all, knew what Adam would do. But Adam's sin did present a problem. How could a sovereign God, in a universe governed by natural law, implement His will in a world under the dominion of a rebel to whom He had given a free will?

There's a question with which theologians have struggled for centuries: How can God be truly sovereign and man truly free? Most have adopted the position that if mankind is free, God is not sovereign; holding to the sovereignty of God, they conclude that mankind isn't really free. It is my conviction that both are possible: Mankind is free and God is sovereign. In fact, I believe it was for this very reason that God established the highest law of the universe—a law that would guarantee His sovereignty and mankind's free will.

Higher Laws

The law of gravity is a high law, but not the highest. I got on an airplane the other day and, though that airplane and its cargo weighed hundreds of tons, it rolled down the runway and climbed to 35,000 feet and came rushing toward my destination at 550 miles per hour. As the pilot gently reduced the speed, we landed on the runway safe and sound, not once breaking the law of gravity. The laws of velocity and aerodynamics worked together to 'overcome' the pull of gravity.

What does this have to do with prayer?

The law of prayer is the highest law of the universe—it can overcome the other laws by sanctioning God's intervention. When implemented properly the law of prayer permits God to exercise His sovereignty in a world under the dominion of a rebel with a free will, in a universe governed by natural law.

There are those among the rebels who have chosen of their own free will to obey God. They want His will to be done more than their own. So they pray, "Thy kingdom come. Thy will be done in earth as in heaven."

As they pray that prayer, they set up the conditions under which God can legally impose His will in a given situation.

Pharaoh did not want to release the people of Israel. It was not his will to do so. It was, however, the will of God. As the people prayed, the Lord sent a deliverer. He intervened in opposition to the will of Pharaoh. As you read through the Scriptures, you see this principle working over and over again.

The Book of Joshua record the story of the Israelites' possessing the land God had promised Abraham as an eternal inheritance. During one fierce battle with the Amorites, they needed more daylight in order to complete the rout. As Joshua consulted with the Lord about the matter, he evidently was told what to do. Joshua came out of the place of prayer and commanded the sun to stand still. It did—for almost a full day according to Joshua 10:13. Joshua, through prayer, determined the will of God about the matter; he was told what to do; he did it and the battle was won. He made it lawful for God to supersede natural law and do what was necessary to extend the length of a day. it happened because a man knew God's will and did it.

You think you need a longer? Don't try it. Joshua did not come up with a bright idea and then ask God to make it work. He got his idea from God. When God tells us to do something, it will be successful, not once in a while, but every time. I do not mean to imply that there will be no problems. The truth is, there may be many problems.

God, Our Leader

Moses was in the will of God when he went to deliver Israel from Egyptian bondage, but it was not an easy task. At times it seemed as though the whole idea was a mistake. just when it seemed they had finally been released and were on their way to the promised land, Pharaoh changed his mind and led his army in pursuit. Behind were the Pharaoh and his army; ahead was the Red Sea. It seemed there was no way out. Something supernatural would have to happen and it did.

Moses was a pray-er, always talking to God, and God was always talking with him. The situation was desperate. They needed a miracle, but not once did Moses tell God what He should do. Moses spoke to the people, who were already complaining: "Do not be afraid. Stand still, and see the salvation of the Lord, which He will accomplish for you today. For the Egyptians whom you see today, you shall see again no more forever" (Ex. 14:13). Then the Lord told Moses what to do: "Life up your rod, and stretch out your hand over the sea and divide it" (14:16). That he did, and the waters parted allowing the whole nation to cross on dry land. Moses' prayer and faith set up the conditions under which God could do what He willed to do. It is not clear whether or not Moses knew exactly what God was going to do, but he knew God would do something.

The prayer of faith makes it possible for God to do what He wills to do. Prayer does not generally change the mind of God, though there have been times when He has changed His stated intention (see next chapter). It more often allows Him to do His will.

Our first building at Church on the Rock was in the very last stages of completion. Announcements of the opening services had gone out and the people were very excited—especially since they were moving in debt-free. Then the city building inspectors came to make a final check before issuing the occupancy permit. Everything was exactly right in the building, but he said the ditch carrying our sewer line to the main line was filled with the wrong size of gravel. On Wednesday before the opening Sunday service, he ordered the ditch to be dug out and the gravel replaced. Machinery was immediately brought in and the work started. It could be completed by Sunday—if the weather cooperated.

Saturday came and everything was going well. It seemed the work would be finished by nightfall. The sky toward the southwest darkened and streaks of lightning were seen—it was raining on Lake Ray Hubbard, only two miles west, coming down in sheets. The rain was headed straight toward Rockwall.

When the rain was less than a mile away, the workmen headed for cover. But the foreman, a member of the church said, "Don't stop. It isn't going to rain on this property today."

Well, it rained west and north of where the work was going on, but not there. Why? "The pastor was praying," the foreman said. Prayer had allowed God to impose His will legally in the matter and move the clouds around.

The "If" Factor

You may ask, Can I change the weather if I pray? Probably not. However, 'if' it is something that will bring glory to God and is a part of His plan, it will be done as we pray. You must understand the 'if' factor, which is always there. God cannot answer every prayer we pray. Not because He does not have the ability, but because it is not His will. Nowhere has God promised to answer every prayer we pray. Things would be in a real mess if He did.

Many years ago the Arkansas football team beat Nebraska in the Cotton Bowl. After the game one of my deacons said, "I knew they were going to win,"

"How did you know that?" I asked.

"I prayed for them." he responded quickly.

"But." I said, "don't you think there were people praying for Nebraska to win?"

"Yes," he answered, "but I prayed first".

Of course he was only joking, but it illustrates a point. If the weather were controlled by people's prayers, we would have serious troubles. Having said that, I wouldn't want you to believe that God cannot change the weather in answer to the prayers of His people. The skeptics may not believe it, but I am sure it has been in the past and will be in the future.

While in Florida, I heard the story of a hurricane that had been heading toward Miami. It was a big one, and if it hit, there was certainly going to be much damage and possibly loss of life. As it neared the coast, many Christians gathered and prayed that the course of the hurricane would be altered. Suddenly it stopped and just remained in the same place for hours as if gathering momentum for an attack. The people kept praying; it was almost as if a battle was going on. Then eventually the winds moved, but not toward to coast. It went to the northeast without causing any serious trouble. Did prayer change things? It set up the conditions under which God could legally alter the course of the storm.

Needed: Prayer

As I grasped this principle, I understood certain Scriptures that previously had made little sense.

Take Matthew 9:36-38, for example: "But when He saw the multitudes, He was moved with compassion for them, because they were weary and scattered, like sheep having no shepherd. Then He said to His disciples, "The harvest truly is plentiful, but the laborers are few. Therefore pray the Lord of the harvest for send out laborers into His harvest."

Jesus saw the multitudes and was moved with compassion. Thank God, we have a savior who has emotions. He felt something when He saw people as sheep having no one to lead them. They were lost, with no sense of direction. As a teenager I often went hunting in the woods, and I know what it is like to think you are at a certain place and then find out that you are lost. Many are lost and do not even know it.

As a result of His compassion for these lost sheep, Jesus told His followers, "The harvest truly is plentiful, but the laborers are few." I am sure He is saying those same words to His followers today—there are more lost sheep than ever. And compared to the magnitude of the harvest, laborers are still scarce.

But Jesus said more. He gave His disciples a strange directive: "Therefore pray that the Lord of the harvest will send laborers into His harvest." Why did He tell us to pray? Surely we can do better than that. If there is a shortage of laborers, why not begin classes on evangelism? Or why not call the best evangelist we can find? Announce an evangelistic crusade. Call in gifted musicians. Spread the word far and wide. Hand out invitations. Knock on every door in the community. We just have to do something about bringing in the harvest. But pray? That is what Jesus said to do. Yes, pray! Pray! Pray! We have done about everything except pray, though we do a little of that also: "Lord, now bless our best efforts, we pray, in Jesus' name. Amen."

All of the above things may be all right, but they are not what Jesus instructed us to do. Perhaps some are saying; I know what Jesus said to do, but it doesn't make good sense. Why do we need to pray about something that is so obviously His will? It is His harvest. His followers are His laborers. If He wants them sent, why doesn't He just send them?

I agree that it doesn't make sense—unless you understand how God implements His will.

Two hundred years ago John Wesley said, "God does nothing but in answer to prayer." Wesley didn't give any further explanation of that statement, and I believed it for years before I understood it: God must wait until He is asked before He can do what He wants to do—not because He is powerless, but because of the way He has chosen to exercise His will.

Jesus was saying, "I want to send laborers, but you must pray. When you pray, I will send."

Ezekiel 36 contains a revelation of this very principle. Her the prophet, speaking in God's behalf, says to the nation of Israel: "I will take you from among the nations, gather you out of all countries, and bring you into your own land. Then I will sprinkle clean water on you, and you shall be clean; I will cleanse you from all your filthiness and from all your idols. I will give you a new heart and put a new spirit within you" (vv. 24-26). After reemphasizing those words, God says, "I, the Lord, have spoken it, and I will do it" (v.36). That is where most of us stop reading, but look at the next verse; "I will also let the house of Israel inquire of Me to do this for them." These things will God do, but not until He is asked.

The same principle is found in James: "You do not have because you do not ask" (4:2). We must pray; it is the only way God can legally intervene.

What I have tried to show in this teaching is that God operated by divine law and established principle; He exercises His will under strict rules. He has chosen to involve us in that process. And to me, that is exciting. We are not pawns on some great chessboard of life to be moved about by forces over which we have no control. We are involved. We are working together with God in the implementation of His holy will. Get these truths in your spirit and your attitude toward life will change. You can make a difference; you can set up the conditions under which things can be changed.

Chapter Nine

Our Response to God

Prophets have always been controversial people—men and women sent by God to speak His word to a generation. How should we Christians respond to prophetic messages of holy people? How should we respond when we hear His voice?

God Spoke and Nothing Happened

I was pasturing a growing church in Arkansas. how I loved that church, the easiest church I had ever served. There were only seventy-five members when they called me. Though I was pastor of a larger church at the time, I felt sure the Lord wanted me to accept their call.

I preached for nearly five months without seeing one person saved. Then, on a Super Bowl Sunday, the Lord saved two people—a boy and a young, well-known businessman. From that day we saw people commit their lives to Jesus, week after week. The building was crowded even with two Sunday morning services.

During those days I heard God speak to me and say, "I am going to raise up a church here of one thousand members." I was sure God had spoken, so I went to the people with that word. They responded positively and soon we were constructing a larger building. Everyone anticipated the completion of that sanctuary, and when the work was finished, we moved into the new facility. We were a congregation of four hundred in a building which seated 750 with the overflow opened, and suddenly things seemed different. The warmth people had felt in the little sanctuary wasn't there. No one had been saved in the new building. No weddings or funerals had been conducted there. Nothing good or bad had happened in that place. None of us understood these feelings, and suddenly I felt pressure to make the church grow, to make things happen.

For the first time I attended a church-growth conference. It seemed as if we should get into the bus ministry. Churches with buses were growing—but not mine. The more I tried to build the attendance, the greater my frustration. Nothing seemed to work. The people complained. The deacons were upset with me but tried not to show it. After nearly three years in the new building, we were still a congregation of four hundred. We questioned the word I supposedly had received from God. Finally I left and so did most of the people.

The question that troubled me for a long time was, Had I heard a word from God? I was sure at the time, and I convinced the people, but it did not happen the way I had been told.

A similar situation occurred when I was serving the Church on the Rock in Rockwall, Texas, as pastor of prayer. Conditions at the Church on the Rock were somewhat like those I had experienced in Arkansas. The church was growing at an unprecedented rate. Ultimately five services were conducted on Sunday to accommodate the crowds. Pastor Larry Lea and the elders decided to build; plans were drawn and construction began.

The people were excited and were giving sacrificially. Pastor Lea believed God had spoken to him: The church was to be built only as fast as money came in. In turn, Pastor Lea told the congregation, "We are going to build by the boot and not by the bank." The 'boot' had been given to him by a cowboy during the first building program. The cowboy had been putting the tithes of his earnings as a rodeo bull-rider into the boot, and the people were so inspired by his gift that they began putting money for the building into it. It became an offering plate of sorts.

The first building was built from money that came through that old boot.

However, as construction proceeded on the new sanctuary, the need for funds was greater than the incoming contributions. Strong appeals were made to the people. Though the offerings were good, they still fell short. The steel was about to be delivered on the site and the payment was over a million dollars. A decision had to be made. Had God spoken? If He had, why this shortage of funds?

Ultimately the decision was made to borrow and the construction proceeded. But many expressed confusion over what had happened.

These two similar experiences prompted my search for some answers. I knew Larry Lea could hear the voice of God. I was sure I had heard God speak to me, but neither thing had happened. Why? At that point God showed me that things do not happen simply because God speaks them. Things happen because the people respond appropriately to what God speaks.

Let me illustrate my point. Jonah was sent by God to Nineveh with a prophetic word. "Yet forty days, and Nineveh shall be overthrown!" (Jon. 3:4). The message offered no way out. Forty days and it is all over. Jonah did not want to go to Nineveh. In spite of the direct word from God, "Go to Nineveh," Jonah took a boat to Tarshish. Jonah did not want to warn the Ninevites because he knew the loving nature of God. He was sure God would not destroy them if they repented, and he wanted those enemies of Israel to be destroyed. With great reluctance Jonah went to Nineveh (after a detour through the belly of a whale). He entered into the city and gave the message.

Just as he expected, they repented. The greatest to the least of them believed the message of the prophet. Even the king laid aside his royal robes, put on sackcloth and sat on the ash heap. The Ninevites said, "Who can tell if God will turn and relent, and turn away from His fierce anger, so that we may not perish?" (3:9). They had no assurance that repenting would help, but they decided to give it a try. They changed their attitude toward God and He changed His mind (stated intentions) There was no change in His nature or His character—He just changed His plans for Nineveh.

Of course Jonah was upset. He looked like a false prophet. His prophecy did not come to pass. Someone has pointed out that Jonah's prophecy of destruction came to pass later, but not in that generation. We are not responsible for the generation past of the one in the future, only the present one.

Before I discuss this further, I want to establish that God makes two kinds of promises. The Bible records a few covenants that are unconditional and irrevocable.

Unconditional Covenants

Consider Malachi 3:6, where God spoke and said, "For I am the Lord, I do not change; therefore you are not consumed, O sons of Jacob." Note carefully what God is saying: "Because I am God and because I do not change, you sons of Jacob are not consumed."

Why was God saying this to Israel? Because He had made an unconditional covenant with Abraham (and renewed it with Isaac and Jacob) that Israel would be blessed and that they would be a blessing to all the peoples on the earth. God's promise to Abraham was, "I will establish my covenant between Me and you and your descendants after you in their generations, for an everlasting covenant, to be God to you and to your descendants after you" (Gen. 17:7).

But hundreds of years had passed. Abraham's descendants were not like Abraham. They were willful, disobedient rebels. To these rebels God said,. "Because I do not change, you are safe. If I did change, you would be consumed. Your sins warrant judgment, but I made a promise to Abraham and I cannot change. If I were a fickle God—as inconsistent and changeable as you—you would be consumed. But I am God. My nature (love) and My character (holiness) never change. Therefore, you have hope."

God had also made an unconditional, irrevocable covenant with Noah and his descendants: "I will never again curse the ground for man's sake, although the imagination of man's heart is evil from his youth; nor will I again destroy every living thing" (Gen. 8:21). Then God said, "This is the sign of the covenant which I make between Me and you, and every living creature that is with you, for perpetual generations: I set my rainbow in the cloud and it shall be a sign of the covenant between Me and the earth…I will look on it (the rainbow) to remember the everlasting covenant between God and every living creature of all flesh that is on the earth" (Gen. 9:12,13,16). Nothing will alter this covenant because God does not change. we can depend on it. His nature and His character are ever the same. This covenant is irrevocable, because it is unconditional.

Conditional Covenants

There are other covenants that are conditional and therefore revocable. Conditional covenants are in force as long as the conditions are met. If we fail to meet the conditions, God has the option to cancel the covenant. However, His very nature often causes Him to extend a covenant even after the conditions stated in the covenant have not been met. An example of this king of covenant is found in Exodus 15:26. Here the Lord says, "If you diligently heed the voice of the

Lord your God and do what is right in His sight, give ear to His commandments and keep all His statutes, I will put none of the diseases on you which I have brought on the Egyptians. For I am the Lord who heals you." Though Israel did not always meet the conditions of this covenant, God was longsuffering toward them. He sent judgment only when there was no alternative.

Many of the promise-covenants of God are conditional. They usually begin with "If you…". The 'if' then covenant is seen in both Old and New Testaments. God says, "If you will, then I will. If you do not, then I will note."

The Power of Prayer

As I was searching the Word for answers to my questions of why a prophetic word doesn't always come to fruition, I read one of Ezekiel's prophecies against the nation of Israel:

The conspiracy of the prophets in her (Israel's) midst is like a roaring lion tearing the prey; they have devoured the people; they have taken treasure and precious things; they have made many widows in her midst. her priests have violated My law…her princes in her midst are like wolves tearing the prey…her prophets…(say), "Thus says the Lord God," when the Lord had not spoken. The people of the land have used oppressions committed robbery, and mistreated the poor and needy…" (Ezek. 22:24-29).

What a broad indictment. The priests, the princes, the prophets and the people were all corrupt and guilty before God. Conditions had deteriorated to the point where something had to be done.

God is the judge of the whole earth. he gave the law and must uphold it. The sentence demanded by the law must be carried out. God is faced with a dilemma. He is love, and He wants to extend mercy. But He is holy and the law demands judgment. How can mercy be extended? How can God delay sending judgment? Verse 30 holds the answer: "I sought for a man among them who would make a wall (hedge), and stand in the gap before Me on behalf of the land, that I should not destroy it; but I found no one." That's it. If there could be found even one person who would intercede for these rebels, God would be able to extend mercy even when judgment was called for. Prayer could provide a way for God to extend His mercy.

Again, it was obvious to me that through prayer God could change things. How sad that in the case of Israel, He found no one who would pray. "Therefore, "the record says, "I have poured out My indignation on them; I have consumed them with the fire of My wrath"(v.31). Anyone can see that this is not what God wanted to do. he had no alternative. There was no other way.

With this truth I searched a little deeper. would God actually change His plan? Would He change His mind? Is the outcome of a matter determined by what God says or by how we 'respond' to what He says? It was not long before I saw that the latter was the case. Things do no happen, altogether, because God says it. Rather things happen because we respond in an appropriate manner to what He says.

At one time God spoke to Jeremiah and said, "Do not pray for this people, or lift up a cry or prayer for them; for I will not hear them in the time that they cry out to Me because of their trouble" (Jer. 11:14). A little later God spoke again, "Do not pray for this people, for their good. When they fast, I will not hear their cry; and when they offer burnt offering and grain offering, I will not accept them" (14:11,12). If these words were not enough to make it clear that He would not hear Israel's prayers or accept their worship, He spoke again and said, "Though Moses and Samuel stood before Me, yet My mind could not be favorable toward this people. Cast them out of My sight" (15:1). However, in spite of all of these words from the Lord telling Jeremiah to cease praying, he prayed all the more. When God says don't pray, it is not the time to stop. He will not disregard the cry of the intercessor.

Jeremiah knew the unchanging nature and the character of God. Knowing that God could change His mind about the matter, he kept praying.

Jeremiah 18 holds the key to understanding how God works. Please read verses 7 and 8 carefully: The instant I speak concerning a nation and concerning a kingdom, to pluck up, to pull down, and to destroy it, if that nation against whom I have spoken turns from its evil, I will relent of the disaster that I thought to bring upon it." Do you hear what God is saying? He is saying, "If the people respond properly, I will change my mind. If they repent, I will repent and relent. It is all up to the people. It does not matter what I have said; I will change My mind—though not My nature or character."

Now let's look at the next two verses: "And the instant I speak concerning a nation and concerning a kingdom, to build and to plant it, if it does evil in My sight so that it does not obey My voice, then I will relent concerning the good which I said I would benefit it" (vv. 9,10).

There was my answer. I began to understand why things do not always happen the way God says they will happen. If He says, "I will build a church here of one thousand people, "it will happen only if we set ourselves in agreement with the word and pray until it happens. If we allow criticism, unbelief, doubt and prayerlessness to take control, the thing God said would happen will not happen.

When God says judgment will fall upon the land, I repent of the sins of the nation and cry to God for mercy. If the prophets say, "Revival is coming," I do not wait for it to happen, If I do, it will not happen. The prayer of faith and repentance are the appropriate response to the prophetic word.

Daniel 9:2 recorded: "I, Daniel, understood by the books (prophecies) the number of the years specified by the word of the Lord, given through Jeremiah the prophet, that He would accomplish seventy years in the desolations of Jerusalem." Daniel knew the time for Israel's return from captivity had come. he had read it in Jeremiah's prophecy. What would he do? He could have told the captives that their days of shame were finished. he could have said, "Deliverance is on the way." But that is not he did. "I set my face toward the Lord God to make request by prayer and supplications, with fasting, sackcloth, and ashes" (v. 3). The next several verses of Daniel 9 are the record of his prayer of repentance for the nation of Israel. He confessed and repented of the sins of the nation as though they were his own personal sins. Daniel responded correctly to Jeremiah' prophecy.

It does not matter what God has said, whether promise of blessing or warning of judgment. If we pray, He will heal our land. If we don't, He won't, even if He has said He would.

Someone may be asking, What will such teaching do to the word of God? I'm more concerned about what it does to one's image of God. We are not serving a molten image. Our God is not a stone. he is a living being who can be touched with our sincere prayers. He will not change His nature or His character, nor will He break His unconditional covenants. But when it comes to holding back judgment or changing His plan about pouring out His wrath, nothing could please Him more. Judgment is never God's plan A; it is always plan B. If judgment comes, it will come because there was no one who would make up the hedge and stand in the gap before the Lord for the land.

My dear reader, we must pray; pray as we have never prayed. The salvation of millions in our generation depends on divine intervention, which cannot happen unless we pray.

CHAPTER TEN

Revival --- God's Response to Prayer

Some time ago J. Sidlow Baxter spoke at the University Baptist Church in Fayetteville, Arkansas. This great English preacher said, "I have pastored only three churches in my years of ministry. We had revival in every one. He continued to say with that beautiful articulation and resonant voice, "And not one of them came as a result of my preaching. They came as the result of a small number of the membership entering into a covenant to pray until revival came. And it did come, every time."

In 1977 I was called to pastor First Assembly of God Church in Kilgore, Texas. It was an old church trying to break out of traditionalism. I preached on the subject of prayer and encouraged the people to pray for revival. In February 1978 a young parishioner came by my office and in the course of the conversation asked, "Pastor, do you know Larry Lea?"

I had heard of him but didn't know him. He then told me that Larry was the youth pastor at Beverly Hills Baptist Church in Dallas. I had heard of that church—almost everyone had in those days. It was then one of the largest charismatic churches in the nation. Their growth, under the late Howard Conatser, had been phenomenal. Larry, I was told, was largely responsible for what had happened there.

This young fellow then said, "Pastor, I think you should pray about having Larry come for a youth meeting here." I followed my brother's counsel, prayed about it and then felt led to call Larry. When I did, he gave me an answer right away. Yes, he would come in July for the youth rally; if things went well, we would follow the rally with a sever-day revival meeting.

I did not meet Larry face to face for two or three more months, when he came to visit his parents who lived in Kilgore. As we sat and talked, our hearts were knit together. His pastor, Howard Conatser, was dying with cancer; Larry needed to talk, and talk we did. Weeks later, after Howard went to be with the Lord, Larry called me and said, "While I was shaving this morning God spoke to me and told me you were to be my pastor. I am to put my ministry under your authority." I will never forget the awesome feeling that came over me that day. I felt as if the greater was bowing and coming under the authority of the lesser. God showed me that Larry would have a great ministry which would affect this whole nation.

Larry and I decided we would not have the rally in July; rather we announced that it would begin the tenth of September and continue as long as we felt led.

Ninety days prior to the meeting the whole church concentrated their prayer toward revival. Then, twenty-one days before the services were to begin, we had prayer twenty-four hours a day. Gaylon Haygood and Joel Pepper, high school seniors, took the hours between one and three in the morning—they were serious and wanted the most difficult shift. Everyone had high expectations; proper ground work had been laid; we had 'prayed the price.'

No one was surprised when several young people were saved the very first night. Among them was the leading football player on the local high school team.

Through prayer and the efforts of Joel and Gaylon the whole senior class was saved. The entire football team in their school came to know Jesus. In all, more than four hundred were saved over the next seven weeks.

For years I had been rising up early in the morning to pray. Larry told me he'd always want to do this, but he didn't have the discipline. During those meetings, I went by his house at 4:45 a.m., and together we went to the place of prayer. It was there, Larry says, that God gave him many of the revelations which led to his life changing teaching on prayer. He saw, firsthand, that revival and prayer are inseparably linked. You cannot have one without the other.

Very soon after that revival I was sitting in my study one Saturday morning when God spoke to me and instructed me to call the nation to prayer—a task that at the time seemed utterly impossible. Who was I? No one knew my name. I explained all of this to the Lord and offered a few suggestions about whom He might get to carry out such a great mission. I remember saying, "You should call Oral Roberts, Rex Humbard, Kenneth Copeland or someone like that. Everyone knows who they are." However, after protesting, I set out to accomplish the mission He had put upon my heart: "Enlist, instruct, encourage and inspire people to pray and give them daily directions in prayer."

I shared this matter with my friend Larry, who showed little enthusiasm for it. But in obedience to the call, I resigned the church, began a radio ministry called "National Call to Prayer" and conducted seminars on the dynamics of prayer. Larry continued to hold evangelistic crusades in which God was moving.

Not quite a year later, a troubled church I had formerly pastored called me, believing I could get things straightened out. I consented to try—and I did what I could but not with any positive results. When I had been there only two or three weeks, Larry called and said, "God has told me to go to Rockwall, Texas, and establish His people there."

With some chagrin, I must say, that I discouraged him. At heart Larry is an evangelist. I couldn't see him pasturing a church. But, after prayer, I knew God had spoken and so consented to lay my hands upon Larry and give him my blessing. That was New Year's Eve 1980. Church on the Rock of Rockwall, Texas, began two weeks later, and from its beginning prayer was the central theme.

Larry and his staff met morning by morning to pray over the church, asking for the Lord's direction. Three years later, I joined the staff as pastor of prayer and counseling. My vision to call the nation to prayer seemed dead. I had failed. I had tried—tried with all my heart—but it had not happened.

As the Church on the Rock was growing phenomenally, pastors across the nation began asking, "What's going on in Rockwall, Texas?" Larry's answer in those days was always the same. Using the words of Paul Yonggi Cho, pastor of the world's largest church, he would say, "We pray and we obey." And that is what we did.

In the winter of 1984, when Larry was called to conduct a prayer clinic in St. Louis, Missouri, the results were more than anyone could expect. From that meeting came Larry's manual 'Could You Not Tarry One Hour?', which has been distributed around the world.

At that meeting Larry saw that he could indeed enlist, instruct, encourage and inspire people to pray. The vision was reborn, this time in the young man I had discipled in prayer. He would get the job done. People in Rockwall, Texas, that was built on nothing more that prayer. Doors opened everywhere for this teaching ministry on prayer. Both Larry and I began receiving invitations to conduct prayer seminars all over the country and in other nations. The call of God has become more specific. He asks that we enlist, instruct, encourage and inspire three hundred thousand righteous pray-ers. That is one-tenth of one percent of the United States population, at the time,--the same percent of the population that God said could have saved the city of Sodom. That army of pray-ers had now been mobilized, praying daily for this nation.

While Larry and I have been enlisting and training people to pray, others have been doing the same thing. Some have been at it longer than we have. God has put this vision in the hearts of many. Some time after that I heard Oral Roberts say, "We've got to get these three hundred thousand pray-ers raised up." Kenneth Copeland was also spending a great deal of time teaching on prayer.

By February 1988 there were fifty thousand or more who had responded to the call to join the army of pray-ers. We had a substantial number of people committed to pray, but how were we going to direct them? This question was troubling no only to me, but leaders of other prayer ministries as well. Television and radio were too expensive and not very effective. The mail was slow and also expensive. Telecommunications would work but were also cost-prohibitive. The Lord had the answer.

Early in the morning of February 7, 1988, the Lord showed me an effective, yet inexpensive way to reach the pray-ers of America and even around the world; by telephone and shortwave radio. "But Lord," I said, "only a small number of people in America listen to shortwave radio."

Then the Lord revealed to me that not everyone needed to listen. If just one in a group of people received daily direction, that person could spread the word. Then He reminded me that the government had grouped all of the people in America in conveniently small groups: zip codes. By sorting the pray-ers by zip codes, we could let each pray-er know of other local prayers. Small groups could then immediately be formed.

We'd ask one person in each zip code to volunteer as a field commander. he or she would purchase a short-wave radio receiver, tune to the proper frequency each day for prayer directives and then share them with each of the pray-ers in his or her group.

The Lord had another word for me. He said that this information was to be gathered, evaluated and disseminated through an office located in Washington, D. C., to be called the National Prayer Embassy.

Over the next three months, I had the opportunity to communicate personally with leader of every major division of the prayer army. I offered them the use of the embassy and the network for contacting their pray-ers.

I believe we are on the threshold of the greatest effort in prayer that the world has ever known. Who knows what the Lord will do as the whole Christian world is united in prayer? Prayer does bring revival. As for me, I can hardly wait to see the Lord's work accomplished.

Chapter Eleven

How Does Doubt Affect Our Prayers?

The question of doubt is an undercurrent I often sense in Christians' struggle with prayer. They wonder if their doubts make their prayers ineffectual.

Doubt is the product of experience. Faith is the product of a relationship with God, which began with a revelation. Doubt and faith live side by side in all of us. Let me point out that every believer will sooner or later have a bout with doubt. Aren't we all doubters by nature? (Those who aren't are called gullible.) If we don't question and doubt, we will run into real trouble. Of course, you are a doubter at times. That's all right. Join the human family. Doubt only becomes a problem when it dominates your like. In short, 'doubt is no hindrance to prayer unless it keeps you from praying.' Most men and women of faith wrestle at times with doubt.

John the Baptist is one of the best examples of a man of faith coming under the power of doubt. Scripture tells us that John was filled with the Holy Spirit from his birth, which itself was miraculous. An austere, ascetic recluse, he lived in the wilderness of Judea—some believe with the Essenes—near the Dead Sea. One day John saw his cousin Jesus coming toward him and cried out with a loud voice, "Behold! The Lamb of God who takes away the sin of the world!" (John 1:29). John knew the true identity of Jesus, His mission and His origin. At Jesus' baptism, John saw the heavens open and the Spirit come down in the form of a dove and rest upon Jesus. He heard a voice from heaven say, "You are MY beloved Son; in You I am well pleased" (Luke 3:22). Concerning Jesus, John declared. "He must increase, but I must decrease" (John 3:30). John knew Jesus, perhaps better than anyone else at that time.

Soon after Jesus began His public ministry, John the Baptist was arrested by Herod. While in prison he heard of the works of Jesus and sent two of his disciples with the question: "Are You the Coming One, or do we look for another?" (Matt. 11:3). John was questioning, doubting. Why? It seems to have to do with his hearing about the 'works' of Jesus. Not the miracles, but the works, the conduct, of Jesus. What troubled him? What produced this doubt?

Perhaps he had heard that Jesus had attended a wedding feast in Cana and had turned water into wine. John had never touched wine—he had been commanded by God to abstain (see Luke 1:156). Jesus was developing a reputation as 'a gluttonous man and a winebibber, a friend of tax collectors and sinners' (Matt. 11:19). Possibly John thought, surely the Son of God would be more holy that I am. Doubt built to the point where he had to be reassured, so he sent two disciples to ask, "Are you really the One?'

Jesus did not answer directly. He said, "Go and tell John… the blind receive their sight and the lame walk; the lepers are cleansed and the deaf hear; the dead are raised up and the poor have the gospel preached to them." Then He added, "And blessed is he who is not offended because of Me" (Matt. 11:4-6).

Yes, believers can doubt. All of us do at times, especially when things don't turn out the way we expected. We prayed for a loved one's healing and she died. A preacher in whom we had great confidence failed. A fellow Christian lied to us and cheated us in a business deal. These things happen, and when they do, doubt rises up within us.

One of the most encouraging stories for doubters is found in Acts: the account of the martyrdom of James the apostle and Peter's subsequent arrest. Luke begins chapter 12 by saying that Herod killed James with the sword and arrested Peter, intending to bring him to trial after the Passover. Herod evidently had the same fate in mind for Peter that he had for James: "Peter was therefore kept in prison"(v.5).

James's untimely death had sent waves of doubt through the Jerusalem church. They had fully expected him to be miraculously delivered from prison. It had happened before. Apostles were special messengers, 'God would deliver' is what the church believed and expected. But now James was dead, and Peter was in prison. What were they going to do?

Knowing a little about human nature, I'm sure there were different courses of action suggested by members of the church. Some probably recommended, "We should appeal to Herod for mercy." But certainly someone said, "Let's pray," because that is what they did. But constant prayer was offered to God for him by the church (v.5). Strange as it may seem, there is no indication that the church prayed for James' life. If they did, their request wasn't granted. However, in Peter's case, a small number gathered at John Mark's house and prayed twenty-four hours a day. Two or three days passed without an answer.

Then, in the middle of the night, an angel unbound Peter, led him out of the prison and disappeared. When Peter realized that it was no dream, he made his way to John Mark's house. Once there, he knocked on the locked gate what enclosed the courtyard. Rhoda, a young girl, answered but became so excited when she recognized Peter's voice that she forgot to unlock the gate. Quickly, she ran into the prayer meeting where she announced Peter's presence.

Notice the response of these faithful pray-ers: "You are beside yourself!" One bright fellow said, "It is his angel," implying that Peter had been executed and his spirit had stopped to say good-bye before going on to glory (v.15). These are the words of doubters. Praying doubters, but doubters, nonetheless.

Peter himself struggled with doubt. Peter was that disciple who answered Jesus—when He asked, "Who do you say that I am?"—with such positive faith: "You are the Christ, the Son of the living God" (Matt. 16:15,16). Later on, this same Peter denied even knowing Jesus. The night of Jesus' arrest, doubt and fear won over Peter's faith—but at other times Peter's faith overcame his doubts.

One day Peter and his partners were washing their nets after a bad night of fishing and Jesus asked permission to use Peter's boat as a platform for teaching the people. After He finished speaking, Jesus said to Peter, "Launch out into the deep and let down your nets for a catch? (Luke 5:4). Peter had a decision to make. Reason and experience told him that the effort would be fruitless. He had fished all night and had caught nothing. Besides, If Jesus knew anything about fishing, He would not have told the fishermen to fish in the deep in the daytime: fish were running in the shallows. Such thoughts must have been in Peter's mind, yet he said, "Nevertheless, at Your word I will let down the net" (v.5).

In effect Peter was saying, "It won't do any good. We won't catch anything, but I will let down the net simply because my Lord has asked me to." Peter obeyed, not anticipating what would happen. As they drew in the net, they could feel that it was full. Peter called James and John, his partners in the business, and they loaded both boats with so many fish they were about to sink. When the catch was secured, Peter fell down before the Lord and said, "Depart from me, for I am a sinful man, O Lord" (v.8). It is not recorded, but I am sure Peter was thinking, I didn't expect to catch a thing, and we have nearly sunk two boats with all the fish.

What can we learn from Peter's experience? Let me put it this way: If you've got enough faith to pray and you've got enough faith to obey—even when you doubt that it will do any good—your prayer and obedience will make a great difference.

Will God hear a doubter's prayer? All I can say is, He did. The pray-ers at John Mark's house were not sure God would deliver Peter, but they knew He could, and they decided to pray until the matter was resolved.

I've heard some Bible teachers say, "You have to believe God will do what you ask Him." Based on Scripture, I must respectfully say, that is not true. Let me give you more examples to support my claim.

One day a leper came to Jesus crying, "If You are willing, You can make me clean" (Mark 1:40). Essentially, that leper was saying, "I don't know if You will, but I know You can." To paraphrase Jesus' answer, He said, "That's good enough. If you believe I can, I will."

Another time Jesus said to two blind men, "Do you believe that I am able to do this?" Their response was, "Yes, Lord." When He saw that they believed He was able. He healed them (Matt. 9:28).

Such is the faith of Abraham. In Romans 4:20,21 we read that Abraham 'did not waver at the promise of God..being fully convinced that what He had promised He was also able to perform."

You only have to believe that God can, and then determine to pray that He will, until the matter is resolved.

These followers of Jesus and pray-ers of the first church of Jerusalem had enough faith to pray. They did not let doubt dominate their lives. Remember: Doubt is a hindrance to prayer only if it keeps you from praying.

CHAPTER TWELVE

How Much Faith Pleases God?

Hebrews 11:6 says, "Without faith it is impossible to please Him (G0d)." Romans 14:23 says, "Whatever is not from faith is sin." These are strong words. Faith is essential; we cannot please God without some amount of it. The writer of Hebrews does not tell us how much faith it takes to please God—just that if we don't have it, we cannot possible please Him.

Most Christians believe they need more faith than they have. But it is my conviction that most people have more faith than they think; they often exercise faith without knowing it.

Paul says in Romans 12:3, "God has dealt (given) to each one (believer) a measure of faith," Once the disciples prayed, "Lord, increase our faith" (Luke 17:5). Though some believers, like Stephen, were 'full' of faith (Acts 6:5), others described as 'weak' in faith (Rom. 14:1). From

These and other scriptures, we can see that there are different quantities and qualities of faith.

In the Gospels, Jesus identified different levels of faith. In Matthew 6:30, to those who were worried about whether or not they would have food to eat or clothing to wear, He said, "O you of 'little' faith."

In Matthew 8:26, to His disciples, who were afraid they were going to be shipwrecked, He said, "O you of little faith."

Jesus used that phrase again with Peter when he began to sink while walking on the water toward Jesus (Matt. 14:23-33). Catching him by the hand, Jesus pointed out that Peter's problem, in addition to doubt, was 'little' faith."

On another occasion, when His disciples were concerned that they had no bread, Jesus once more spoke about the smallness of their faith (Matt. 16:80. This time He referred to their lack of understanding of spiritual truth.

In contrast, the Canaanite woman who pleaded for her daughter's deliverance was said to have 'great' faith (Matt. 15:28). And to the centurion who believed Jesus could heal his servant just by speaking the word, Jesus said, "I have not found such great faith, not even in Israel!" (Matt. 5:10).

Jesus identified four kinds of soil in the parable of the sower (see Matt. 13:3-23). Faith is like a seed planted in the soil of a soul. This seed of faith has the potential to grow, and under the proper conditions it may grow quite rapidly. There are circumstances and conditions that are conducive to the growth and development of faith.

On the other hand, there are conditions that are not conducive to the growth of faith. The seed of faith has the potential to grow, yet it does not grow at the same rate in all of us. Even the good soil did not produce all its yield at the same rate. There are conditions and circumstances under which seed planted in good soil will hardly grow. This is true in the natural realm, and anything that is true in the natural realm has its parallel truth in the spiritual realm. Extremely dry conditions stunt growth, and storms and weeds can retard growth—even though there is nothing wrong with the seed, the sower or the soil.

From experience I have learned that the level and quality of faith cannot be determined by one's ability to heal the sick or cast out devils.

Hear the words of Jesus recorded in Matthew 7:21-23: "Not all who sound religious are really godly people. They may refer to Me as 'Lord,' but they still won't get to heaven. For the decisive element is whether or not they obey the Father in heaven. Tt the judgment many will tell Me, 'Lord,

Lord, we told others about You and used Your name to cast out demons and to many other great miracles. 'But I will reply, 'You have never been Mine. Go away, for your deeds are evil'" (author's paraphrase).

Faith's Best Evidence

One's testimony is not the best evidence of faith. Obedience to God's Word and positive action, based on a true conviction that He is and that He can do anything He promised, are faith's best evidence.

A story in Mark chapter 2 has always intrigued me. Jesus was teaching in a certain house in Capernaum. A crowd of people gathered in the house, and when it was full, they filled the yard surrounding the house. These were the conditions facing the four men who came carrying their paralytic friend to the Lord to be healed. There was no room inside or out. Confronted with such a situation, many would have been discouraged and given up, but not these men. Their friend's only hope was in the middle of that crowd, and they had to get him into the presence of Jesus. The only way seemed to be through the roof of the house. It was no small task, but with some difficulty they got their friend onto the roof and began breaking a hole through the tile.

Can't you imagine what was happening down below? Dirt and debris were falling down on the crowd of people, who were none too pleased. Eventually, four faces appeared in the opened hole, and down came the man on a bed into the presence of the Lord. Mark records that Jesus 'saw their faith'. How? Well, you can't really see faith; you can see only what it produces. Jesus called their action, faith. James 2:20 says, "Faith without appropriate action is dead" (author's paraphrase). Unless faith is followed by action, it is an empty confession, often based on presumption.

Someone has rightly said that 'talk is cheap.' Just draw air into your lungs, put pressure on your diaphragm, release a little of that air through your vocal chords, move your lips and tongue, and you can say, "I have great faith." It does not take much to do that, but God's Word makes it clear that He is looking for obedience: "Be doers of the word, and not hearers only" (James 1:2).

If you are a Christian, you have faith. From Hebrews 11:6 we can see how much faith it takes to please God. Hear these words: "He who comes to God must believe that He is..." To please God you must believe that He is. Can you say with confidence, I believe God 'is'? If you can, you have passed the first half of the test. Faith is a deep conviction that, though I have never seen Him with these fleshly eyes, He is. That is what all of the stalwarts of faith listed in Hebrew 11 had that made them different. They all could say, I believe God 'is', not was or will be, but 'is'. I cannot prove it but I know, God is! His name is I AM. Do you believe He is? If you do, then you have faith.

There's an additional characteristic of faith given in verse 6: "For he who comes to God must believe...that He is a rewarder of those who diligently seek Him." The second question on the faith test is: Do you believe that God is a rewarder of those who diligently seek Him? I have asked that question of many people, and most of the answer with a resounding yes. Christians believe that God is, and that He has power to do what He wants to do. No one can please God who does not have this much faith. Can you say, from the heart, I believe God rewards those who diligently seek Him? If you can, you have enough faith to please God.

This kind of faith keeps moving us to action. I cannot believe God is and live as if He is not. My actions will ultimately come into line with my faith. If it is other-wise, I do not have living, active faith. I have only an empty, meaningless, hypocritical profession. James gives us a strong corrective word on this subject: "Dear brothers, what's the use of saying that you have faith and are Christians if you aren't proving it by helping others? Will that kind of faith save anyone?...It isn't enough just to have faith. You must also do good..." (2:14,17, TLB).

Again, if you believe that God is and that He answers those who earnestly call upon Him, you have enough faith to please God. But if that faith is not moving you to do right, you still have a long way to go. People are not displeasing God because of their lack of faith. The thing that has always displeased God is our failure to live out in our daily walk what we say we believe. Faith, real faith, followed by appropriate action is the thing that pleases Him.

What is God's Reward?

God's special favor does not rest upon transgressors, yet God's grace is extended toward all, the just and the unjust, good and bad. All receive sunshine and rain, seedtime and harvest. People do not live because they are good or die because they are bad. Both good and bad enjoy the same opportunities.

Recently a man who was showing me his property said to me, "The Lord has surely been good to me." My response was, "The harder and smarter one works, the more that person seems to be blessed." He was a hard-working, diligent man, and he had material things to show for it. However, the things he had did not come as an indication of God's special favor upon his life. The things he had were the reward of his own personal efforts.

You may disagree with that statement, but please hear me. Yes, I thank the Lord every day for the grace that He has bestowed upon us all. He created us in His image and likeness. There is something of the divine in all of us, good or bad, obedient or disobedient. We have the potential to succeed or fail.

Too often we blame God or the devil for things that are our own doing. And we shouldn't assume that wealthy, seemingly successful people are necessarily walking in God's special favor.

I was in Washington, D.C., working with a realtor who was helping me find property suitable for the National Prayer Embassy. The man was from India, and he'd come to America with eight dollars and seven pounds of clothing. He'd taken a job handling newspapers, working his way through school and is now one of the top men in a very large company. He is not a Christian. Has his success come as a result of God's special favor? I think not.

My dad had only a third-grade education. In spite of his educational deficiency, through hard work and diligence, he established his own business and lived in retirement for more than thirty years on the fruit of his labors. Given the right opportunity, most of us have the ability to get wealth.

All five of my father's sons—raised under the same circumstances, with the same parents—had essentially the same opportunities. Yet we do not all have the same material wealth. If God's special favor can be measured in terms of material wealth, one would have to conclude that God's special favor comes to the unjust more that the just, to the unfaithful rather than the faithful. God's approval on our lives cannot be determined by the quantity of our material possessions.

Without faith we cannot please Him, regardless of what we do. On the other hand, we cannot please Him with a faith that does not move us to right doing. And if we try to measure the favor of God by what we possess, we will live in constant confusion.

Sometime ago I was walking through a new home of a friend. It was nice—a real mansion—and I said to the Lord, "You have really blessed my friend."

I was surprised when the Lord responded, "This is not My blessing."

"Well, Lord, we have always said that these things are blessings from You."

"You don't have anything like this, do you?" He replied.

"Well, no, I don't."

Then God asked, "Do you think I love your friend more that I love you?"

"No, Lord, I know You love me as much as You love him."

God continued, "I do not bless My people with these kinds of things. MY blessings are spiritual blessings."

Then I remembered the words of Paul: "Blessed be the God and Father of our Lord Jesus Christ, who has blessed us with all 'spiritual' blessings in heavenly places in Christ" (Eph. 1:3, italics added).

At that time the Lord said to me, "Material wealth that comes to Christians comes to test their integrity and character. If they use their wealth selfishly, they fail the test." God does not send special favor upon the selfish and self-centered. May friend has wealth because he has worked hard, taken advantage of opportunities and handled his money wisely. It was not the special favor of God. If he does not use this wealth properly, he will answer to God.

As Christians, we are slaves with a Master whose name is Jesus. When I work, it is for Him. When I invest, it is not for me, it is for Him. I have been given some talents to hold or to invest in His behalf. If I become possessive or claim ownership, I have failed the test.

Obedience is better than sacrifice or worship (see I Sam. 15:22). That is what Samuel said to Saul as he returned home with the spoils of battle and the captured King Agag. His orders had been to destroy everything, but

Saul made a decision to disobey; he had a better plan—much more reasonable and logical. And it eventually cost him the kingdom.

Wise Solomon knew that "there is a way which seems right to a man, but its end is the way of death" (Prov. 14:12). God is not interested in our worship if we are walking in disobedience. We must repent and turn from our ways to His. He will forgive, and His special favor can be upon us once again.

Faith in God

What does all of this have to do with prayer? Faith and prayer are vitally linked—not faith in prayer, but faith in God. If you believe God is and that God can, and if you are walking in obedience to His word, you are ready to pray. But pray with faith in God, not with faith in prayer.

H. Clay Trumball, in his little book "Prayer", written nearly a hundred years ago, said:

There is a vast difference between prayer in faith and faith in prayer. Faith in prayer is very common. Almost everybody has more or less of it. Prayer in faith is anything but common; so uncommon, in fact that our Lord questions if He will find any of it when He comes back again to the earth. Prayer in faith is a commanded duty; faith in prayer is not commanded, nor is it justifiable. Prayer in faith is spiritual; faith in prayer, too often, superstitious and presuming.

We must have our faith in God—not in anything we do as a religious act. It is presumptuous to think that we will be heard if we pray just right. Faith in "just right" prayer will not accomplish anything. Our faith must rest in a loving God who hears the prayers of His children and knows when and how to answer. He also knows if they should be answered. When we pray a prayer known to be in the will of God, believing it will be answered, it is. Not some of the time—every time. When we pray not knowing God's will, we ask him to do what He deems best. As we pray with this king of faith, we know that whatever happens, whatever the outcome, His will has been done.

Much of the time our faith in God is not lacking. Rather our problem lies in the fact that we are trying to have faith in ourselves. We mistakenly think we need to pray better prayers to be heard. But faith, if it is to be effective, must rest solely upon the Lord. It must rest in His goodness, not in ours, as I have said before. We must be obedient, but we must not trust in our obedience. We must be righteous, but we cannot trust our righteousness to open heaven to our prayers.

Jesus made this very clear in His story to some who boasted of their virtue:

Two men went up to the temple to pray, on a Pharisee and the other a tax collector. The Pharisee stood and prayed thus with himself: "God, I think You that I am not like other men—extortioners, unjust, adulterers, or even as this tax collector. I fast twice a week; I give tithes of all that I possess." And the tax collector, standing afar off, would not so much as raise his eyes to heaven, but beat his breast, saying, "God be merciful to me a sinner!" I tell you, this man went down to his house justified rather than the other (Luke 18:10-14).

In the eyes of man, the Pharisee was righteous; in the eyes of God, he was a sinner. On another occasion Jesus said, "Many who are first will be last, and the last first" (Matt 19:30).

Spiritual pride and haughtiness will not only separate us from people, these things also put a barrier between us and God. James warns us: "God…sets Himself against the proud and haughty" (4:6, TLB).

It may be that we do not need more faith in either God or ourselves. What we need is greater faithfulness—faithfulness in the place of prayer, faithfulness in the place of worship and praise, faithfulness in the home and in the workplace. God places a high premium on faithfulness. Heaven's rewards are not promised to the successful but to the faithful. That one who seeks God with a pure heart will find Him.

Is Healing Dependent on Great Faith?

While I'm discussing this matter of faith, let me touch upon the matter of prayer for healing. I cannot tell you why God heals one and does not heal another. To say that it is His will to heal everyone, every time, does not seem to measure up to the way things really are. It has been my experience that God, at present, heals some of the people some of the time. Faith, though required to please God, seems to have little to do with it. I have seem people healed who confessed to having no faith. I have seen people who seemed to have deep faith see no positive response to their prayers.

Why are Christians who believe in divine healing sick? It is not necessarily because they have sinned, lost faith or displeased God. Nor is it because God does not heal today. Christians are sick for many of the same reasons others are sick: They were born with physical weaknesses; they have disregarded the laws that govern health; they hold unforgiveness in their hearts; jealousy, bitterness, resentment and fear have weakened their immune systems; low self-esteem and feelings of guilt have produced anxiety.

What is the appropriate response to God's promise "I am the Lord who heals you" (Ex. 15:16)? What about "By His stripes we are healed" (Is. 53:5)? Receive them; believe them. Pray and receive prayer—for divine healing with faith that God can do what you are asking. And if He does not, He is still God; know that as you pray, what happens is the will of God for your life. We must do what we believe we should, and have the attitude of Esther who said, "If I perish, I perish" (Esth. 4:16). I do not always know what is going to happen when I pray. Often I am surprised at the answers, yet I have a made-up mind: I will pray as long as there is life. And in death as in life, I will say, "Nevertheless, Thy will be done."

I hear someone asking, But what about the suffering? Isn't God concerned about pain and death? Does He want His people to suffer?

The Scripture is clear about God's attitude toward to death of a saint: "Precious in the sight of the Lord is the death of His saints" (Ps. 116:15).

Though it is not always easy to see the benefits of suffering, we must believe there are some. Paul said he sought the Lord three times about a problem in his flesh. Then the Lord spoke to him and said, "No, I will not take away the thorn, but I am with you, and that is all you need. My power shows up best in weak people" (see 2

Cor. 12:7-10). Paul learned to say, "When I am weak, then I am strong" the less we have the more we depend on Him.

Greater praise to God comes from those who are delivered out of troubles than those who are shielded from trouble, trial or sickness. The mentality of the early church toward trails and persecution can be seen in Acts 5: Paul said in his letter to the Roman Christians, "I consider that the sufferings of this present time are not worthy to be compared with the glory which shall be revealed in us" (8:18); he added, "All things work together for good to those who love God" (8:28).

In the midst of trouble Romans 8:28 is hard to believe, but looking back from the mountaintop of victory, we can understand it. Every turn in the road was important. Every obstacle overcome made us stronger. Each thing built upon another—all were needed—to bring us to the place we are now. Some of us who are older can look down from the top and say, "Come on, you are going to make it." to those who are about to lose heart. We have been where you are. We made it and so can you: "Let us not grow weary while doing good, for in due season we shall reap it we do not lose heart" (Gal. 6:9).

CHAPTER THIRTEEN

How Should We Pray?

A few years ago I was in Northern Virginia preaching in a small church that met in rooms over an automobile body shop. There may have been two hundred present—including the children, who were personally involved in the service—expressing their joy through dancing. I quickly saw that this was no ordinary church. The pastor sat in the congregation until time to introduce me. The people were free to express worship in any way they chose. The congregation represented a wide cross-section of society: rich and poor; black, white, and Hispanic. When I stood to speak I asked, "How many of you are professional people?" Several raised their hands. "How many own your own businesses?" Others responded. "What in the world are you doing here in this place, when most of you came right by beautiful churches with tall steeples? Why come here?" They spontaneously clapped their hands. They knew the question was rhetorical; we all knew that the presence of the Lord had brought them there to worship.

After the service I was introduced to a woman who told me she had just returned from a mission trip to Nigeria. While there in Africa she had listened to a tape on which I led in prayer. She had prayed along repeatedly, daily. She said that as she followed the prayer some wonderful things happened. Her work went smoothly. Everything seemed to fall into place. She was convinced that Christians should pray this prayer every day.

The prayer I prayed was an expansion of the Lord's prayer (see Matt. 6:9-13). We have evidence that the early church followed the pattern of prayer that Jesus had given them. After Jesus' ascension about 120 disciples prayed as they waited for the coming of the Holy Spirit. Concerning them the record states, "These all continued with one accord in prayer and supplication, with the women and Mary, the mother of Jesus, and with His brothers" (Acts 1:14). In the original Greek the first part of this passage reads, "These all continued in…'the' prayer." In my opinion, 'the' prayer could have been none other than the prayer Jesus gave them to pray.

Everything about which Christians need to pray is covered under the various points of this prayer outline:

"Our Father"--- speaks of relationship.

"Which art in heaven"--- reminds us of His sovereignty.

"Hallowed by thy name"--- leads us to praise.

"Thy kingdom come"--- puts first things in first place.

"Thy will be done"--- releases everything to His control.

"Give us"--- He is our source; we are needy.

"This day"--- reminds us to be consistent.

"Our daily bread"--- Jesus is the bread of life.

"Forgive us"--- reminds me of my sins and His solution.

"As we forgive"--- keeps me free from unforgiveness.

"Lead us"--- His Spirit leads.

` "Not into temptation"--- temptation is real

"Deliver us from the evil one"--- through Jesus I will overcome.

"Thine is the kingdom"--- divine ownership.

"Thine is the power"--- full authority.

"Thine is the glory"--- return to praise.

(For an excellent teaching on this prayer, read Larry Lea's 'Could You Not Tarry One Hour?' (Creation House).

An Example

To show you how you might fill in this outline, I will write out this prayer exactly as I pray it. Of course I don't say the same words every day; but I follow this pattern, which I trust will help you as much as it helped the woman I met in Virginia. This prayer will set up the conditions under which God has the option to do anything that needs to be done.

Father, You are in heaven, over all the things of this earth. You see all. You are concerned about all. I thank You that I can call You my Father. You are my Father. You chose me, Father, out from among all the others, and You marked me out to be an exact duplicate of Your Son, Jesus. Thank You, Father. You cleansed me from all of my sins. I enter into Your presence only because You offered a sacrifice for my sins. Through that sacrifice, I can come boldly to the throne of grace. Thank You, Father, that we do not come to a throne of judgment; we come to a throne of grace. I will not be rejected. I am accepted in Christ Jesus, my Lord, whose blood has atoned for my sins. I come before You, not with a righteousness I have attained through self-effort, but in a righteousness I obtained by faith—the righteousness You provide. I am accepted, not because I am good, but because you are good. You are my righteousness. Through the blood I have forgiveness of sins. And not only do I have forgiveness of sins through the blood, I have the fullness of the Holy Spirit.

Thank You, Father, for the indwelling presence of the person of the Holy Spirit. He is my peace. He is my glory. What a blessing it is to fellowship with Him. Thank You, Holy Spirit, for living in me. You are welcome in this temple. Take full control of every member of my body. Help me to pray with the spirit and with the understanding.

Father, I thank You that my sins are forgiven and for the fullness of the Holy Spirit, and I thank You that I have soundness of body through the Lord Jesus Christ. With His stripes I am healed. Thank You that healing is not only for me; it is for Your body, the church. Lord , let the healing flow to Your body. Heal the wounds. Bind up the broken ones. Bring unity into Your body.

Thank You, Father, that through the sacrifice You made for us, every financial need is met. You are my provider. You are 'Jehovah-Jireh'. All my needs You have supplied according to Your riches in glory by Christ Jesus, our Lord.

And Father, I thank You that You are my assurance. I will conquer every foe with You on my side. You are my shepherd. I shall not want. You make me to lie down in green pastures. You lead me beside still waters. You restore my soul. You lead me in paths of righteousness for Your name's sake. Though I walk through the valley of the shadow of death, I will fear no evil. Your rod and Your staff comfort me. You prepare a table before me in the presence of my enemies. You anoint my head with oil. My cup is running over. Surely goodness and mercy will follow me all the days of my life, and I will dwell in the house of the Lord, forever and forever. Hallelujah!

Every moral need, every spiritual need, every physical need, every financial need and every emotional need are met in my Lord Jesus. Thank You, Lord, for the provision You have made.

And now, Father, I pray, Thy kingdom come. Thy will be done in earth as it is in heaven. Father, this is what I desire. I want Your kingdom, and You as king to be first in my life. No one but Jesus will rule my life this day. I surrender my whole being to Your lordship. Let Your kingdom be established in my life. Let Your will be done in my life and in my family.

Lord, I lift up my family to you. I pray that each one of my brothers, each one of my children, each one of my grandchildren will let Jesus rule their lives. And, Lord, it is not just for my family that I pray; I pray for my church family.

I pray for my pastor and all the pastors of Your church. May Your kingdom be established and Your will be done in their lives. I stand against the spirit of deception and the spirit of distraction. I bind the spirit of disruption, discouragement and destruction. And, Father, make Your pastors wise. Help them to discern the true nature of every matter. Grant them physical strength to do the work You called them to do.

Father, I pray for all those in leadership in Your church. The elders and deacons—bless them and strengthen them. Grant them the ability to do what You want them to do. Minister to their families, I pray, in Jesus' name.

Not only for the pastors and leaders, Lord, I pray also for the people of Your church. I pray first for the children. Minister to the children of the church and of this generation. Most of them know nothing of Jesus. Raise up strong, effective ministry to the little ones. Raise up and gift people to write and produce television materials suitable for children—programs with the message of hope that are so good, so well produced that the national networks can't reject them.

We lift up the youth to You, O Lord. Reach them, O Lord. Do what must be done to reach them, I pray. Bless and strengthen those who are ministering effectively to the youth of this generation. Supply all of their needs. Open doors for them. Send a manifestation of Your supernatural power. For their sakes, reach them. O Lord.

For the single adults, I pray. Many are hurting. Many suffer from rejection. Many have lost all confidence in themselves. Many are full of anger and bitterness. Minister to them, Lord. Help them to turn their eyes to You. Let Your peace flow through their hearts.

And for the young married ones, I pray, Lord. They need Your help. I stand against the enemy in their behalf. I resist the spirit of destruction that has been sent to destroy marriage relationships today. I resist that spirit in the name of Jesus.

Father, I also pray for senior adults. They need You, Lord. Many feel discouraged. Many have been neglected. Be near them, O Lord, and let them know the reality of Your holy presence.

And Father, I pray for the ministries of the church. For our missionaries, for the evangelists, for teachers we pray. Minister to and through these.

Father, I especially pray for the pray-ers—those upon whom You have placed a desire to pray. Grant that they will never grow weary and lose heart. Help them to pray and to keep on praying until we see the spiritual awakening You promised in Your Word and through Your prophets.

Father, we pray for our nation. We repent of our national sins. We have sinned against You, O Lord. We have legalized the killing of our unborn children. I know this is an abomination in Your sight. We have made it unlawful for our children to pray in the public schools. Forgive us, O Lord. Our sins are many. We repent for those who do not know to repent for themselves. Hear us, O God, and answer and forgive. Send a spiritual awakening. Send those signs Joel spoke of—signs in the heavens above and in the earth beneath; blood, fire and pillars of smoke. Let the sun be darkened and let the moon turn to blood. Let the unbelievers be shocked out of their complacency. Hear, O Lord, and answer. I pray this in the name of Jesus.

I lift up our president and his cabinet. Let Your will be done in them. I pray for the Congress. May each member be led to do right. I pray for the Supreme Court. Watch over the decisions they are called upon to make. Cause them to judge righteously. I lift up the commanders of our armed forces and all of our military personnel. Let there be peace and not war, we pray in Jesus' name.

And now, Lord, I pray: Give us this day our daily bread. You are my source. My needs are supplied by Your hand, Lord, and I thank You. You are the bread of life. I need You to live. Thank You, Jesus, for life through the bread You supply.

Forgive us, Lord, as we forgive others. I confess my sins to You, O Lord. Forgive, I pray. I have set my heart to forgive. I will not take offense today. I have been forgiven and I will forgive, no matter what anyone may do to me. I choose to forgive.

Lead us, Lord, not into temptation. Keep us from being led into wrong paths, I pray. I thank You that we are being led by the Holy Spirit, who lives within us. I have been led, I am being led and I will be led.

Deliver us from the evil one, Lord Jesus. Keep us alert. Point out the evil one's traps. Let us not be overcome of the devil, but rather to overcome—to tread on the serpent, to walk in victory.

I stand with my loins girded about with the truth. I have on the breastplate of righteousness—Your righteousness, Lord, not mine. My feet are shod with the gospel of peace. I have the shield of faith, the helmet of salvation and the sword of the Spirit.

I will pray always with all prayer and supplication in the Spirit for all men. I will walk in victory through the power of the Holy Spirit, declaring that:

Thine is the kingdom.

Thine is the power.

Thine is the glory—forever—amen.

Praise the Lord!

Living Praise

Several years ago I learned how important it is to live in an attitude of praise. David said, "I will praise the Lord at all times; His praise shall continually be in my mouth" (Ps. 34:1). The Living Bible says, "I will praise the Lord no matter what happens". David is saying that he had made a 'conscious decision' to praise the Lord in every circumstance of life. Likewise, we must decide to praise the Lord no matter what happens. I can do this because when I have prayed with all my heart, "Thy kingdom come. Thy will be done," I know whatever happens will be in the will of God.

I remember when this truth became very real to my spirit. I awoke one morning before it was time to arise. God sometimes uses unusual means to teach us. I had two experiences which may seem strange to you. In fact, they seem strange to me, but I will share them with you as they happened since they served to teach me an important lesson. While there in bed, I seemed to hear a conversation going on in heaven. The Father was speaking to another heavenly being about me. He said, "How is it that you do not chastise Willhite?" The other being replied, "Well, every time I do something to correct him, he blames the devil or calls it 'one of those things which happen in life' and he is not helped, so I have decided to let him alone." I was wide awake by the time that conversation was finished. I praised God for everything that had happened to me, both good and bad. I knew that nothing could happen without His permission, so I began to see all things as being in my best interest.

Not long afterward, I awoke again before it was time to get up. This time I seemed to hear a conversation in Satan's headquarters. He was asking a demon, "Why aren't you giving Willhite a hard time?" The demon replied, "Since his eyes were opened about praise, every time I do something to him, he just starts to praise the Lord. I know you don't want him doing that, so I have had to let up on him."

Hallelujah! There is victory in praising the Lord. Praise and intelligent thanksgiving now make up the major part of my prayers. When you praise the Lord, even if you know that Satan is responsible for the problem or difficulty, you put Satan in a bind.

Remember the story of Paul and Silas in prison? They had been beaten and thrown into a dungeon, but at midnight they prayed and sang praises. Satan had put them in that prison, or at least he had moved on the people who served as his agents to do so. All Paul and Silas had done was cast evil spirits out of a little girl. If that had been our crime, most of us would have been complaining in that dungeon. But Paul had learned the secret of walking in victory. All things were working together for his good. He could practice what he wrote to the church at Thessalonica: "In everything give thanks" (1 Thess. 5:28). Paul practiced what he preached. He and Silas were living victoriously in the midst of suffering.

Because of this revelation and a determination to walk in praise daily, I walk in victory most of the time; so can you.

It is so easy to see how the Lord has led our lives when we look back. When you pray to be led by the Spirit, believe me, you are led. Paul says, "A;; who are led by the Spirit of God are sons of God" (Rom. 8:14, TLB). Any way you put it, sons of God are led by the Spirit of God—not by a pillar of fire or a cloud, not even by a voice. His Spirit is in us. We have an internal guidance system. We cannot miss His will or plan for our lives unless we rebel against His revealed will. We are being led. Believe that and you can praise God in every situation.

Your Father may not set you down and talk to you every day, but if you go wrong, you will hear His voice saying, "This is the way, walk in it" (see Is. 30:21). He loves you enough to be with you whichever way you go. To His disciples Jesus says, "Go into all the world and preach the gospel" (Mark 16:15), adding His promise, "I am with you always" (Matt. 28:20). If you go north, He will be there; go south and He will be with you. But He warns us, "If I tell you to go one direction and you go another, you will miss My presence." Though He will never leave us nor forsake us, if we turn left when He says right, we will miss His best plan for our lives. If that happens, we should repent of our disobedience and follow His leading.

So bless the Lord at all times. Let His praise fill your mouth. Trust that He is guiding you; rejoice when things go well and when they go badly. Keep saying and believing that 'all' things work together for your good, and you will walk in victory every day. As David said, "Serve the Lord with gladness; come before His presence with singing....Enter into His gates with thanksgiving, and into His courts with praise" (Ps. 100:2,4). You cannot be defeated when you walk in this truth.

Conclusion

In his book titled 'Concerts of Prayer'. David Bryant said, "I believe that the destiny of a movement of united prayer could result not only in a reprieve of God's stroke of judgment on the developed world, but the unleashing of spiritual power in the church worldwide to carry the gospel forward in an unprecedented manner." Many of us who have been involved in calling the nations to prayer have the same conviction.

We need not only to pray; we need to pray more intelligently. We need to pray with greater understanding, knowing how prayer affects the outcome of things. It is my earnest prayer that the lessons I have shared will give you new insight. Let me repeat what James, Jesus' brother said: "The fervent effectual prayer of a righteous person releases tremendous power" (5:16, author's paraphrase). 'Your prayers are important'. No one has a more privileged access to the throne of God than you do. We all come into His presence in the same manner. By the blood of Jesus we have access to the holiest place of all—the throne of God. (see Heb. 10:19).

It is not necessary for you to send your prayer requests to me or to some prayer warrior. You can pray as effectually as anyone else on earth. Bring your needs to Him. He will hear and He will answer when it is in your best interest to do so.

May His special favor be upon you as you walk with Him in the school of prayer.

One final thought...

If you have purchased this book on Amazon and it makes a difference in your life ... please consider writing a review to encourage others in their search for answers.

Printed in Great Britain
by Amazon

40100709R10096